Hillside Building
Design and Construction
2nd Edition

Published and Distributed By
BUILDER'S BOOK, INC.
BOOKSTORE
1-800-273-7375

Hillside Building
Design and Construction
2nd Edition

Arthur H. Levin

Published and Distributed By
BUILDER'S BOOK, INC.
BOOKSTORE
1-800-273-7375

Cataloguing in Publication
Data

Hillside building design and
construction
by Arthur H. Levin
Includes index.
1. Architectural design
2. Hillside design and construction.
I. Levin, Arthur H.
II. Title.

Library of Congress Catalog
ISBN 1-889892-19-X

Second edition
Printed in the United States

Designed by Builder's Book, Inc.
1-800-273-7375

Caution

This book is intended as a general introduction to basic principles of hillside design and construction for architects, engineers, contractors, and lay people. Many variables can affect
application of these principles to particular projects.
Inadequate understanding of and planning for project specific
circumstances can result in construction that is unsound and
unsafe. Each user must exercise independent judgment to
decide whether, and how, information in the book might apply
to particular projects. Above all, no project should be built with
out thorough evaluation and approval by a licensed civil
engineer or architect.

Contents

Foreword

Building in the hills is an enterprise full of unpleasant surprises and traps just waiting to snare the inexperienced. A book that clarifies and simplifies the process is long overdue. No one I can think of is more qualified to write that book than Art Levin, who, as a structural engineer since 1956, has been involved in more than 2,000 hillside projects, 200 of them as architect as well as engineer.

Art's stated purpose was to write a book that would help the uninitiated to avoid the otherwise inevitable pitfalls and traps. He has succeeded. The book leads the reader in clear, direct prose and logical organization through every step of the complicated process: from evaluating and choosing a hillside site to geological analysis, site preparation, the permit-variance problems, engineering, designing, to contracting and construction—all subdivided and applied to the three hillside site conditions, uphill, downhill, and terraced lots.

Art has gone extensively into the various types of foundation and framing systems appropriate to different soil and site conditions, explaining them and the other structural elements distinct to hillside building. More than 170 excellent line drawings amplify the text graphically.

The book has many real life examples of unexpected encounters with unstable land, surface drainage problems, subterranean water, exigent owners, uncooperative building inspectors, and inexperienced contractors, and other accounts of the author's triumphs and occasional enlightening failures. All of these brief histories are instructive and guaranteed to be of invaluable help to the first or second time designer and builder. Even the experienced reader will learn from Art's step by step exposition of the problems of hillside building, his tips and cautionary tales.

Not the least of the helpful sections of this handbook for hillside building is the section outlining the tasks and responsibilities of the members of the team: the architect, surveyor, soils-geology consultant, structural engineer, civil engineer, and landscape architect.

Reading the manuscript brought back memories of the many projects we have done in the hills over the past 60 years or so, starting with my father Richard Neutra's pioneering effort in this genre, the Lovell Health House of 1929, which is a steel-framed, three-level structure perched on a hillside near Griffith Park, Los Angeles. The building was an ultra-modern, health enhancing design, using light steel members, gunite, a suspended swimming pool, and a number of, for that time, revolutionary approaches. The entire steel frame for this large, multi-level dwelling "laboratory" was erected in one week, and almost all of the concrete had to be conveyed from the street 100 feet away by gunite, the only pump technology known at the time.

For the Health House, foundation design had to be done without the benefit of the then just emerging science of geo-technics or soil engineering, as it is commonly referred to now. It is nothing short of amazing, and a real tribute to those early pioneers, that this building has withstood the major earth-quakes of Long Beach, Sylmar, and Whittier, and innumerable minor temblors, without evidence of distress, except for the lowest stair which reaches grade. All this with a design which predates the Field Act and other earthquake codes.

This illustrates a point that often comes up with
prospects who contact our office. We are asked
about older buildings we may have produced under
previous code editions, such as the cantilever plat-
form structures (on which we collaborated with Art
Levin) above Beverly Glen Blvd. in Sherman Oaks,
California (see Figure 59 and related text). Someone wanting to buy such a house will ask, "Is this
structure earthquake proof?" The answer is, of
course, that no building is earthquake proof, only
relatively earthquake resistant. Thus, as Art men-
tions, it is really the client's choice as to whether he
asks his designers to simply design to current code
practice or to exceed it by some percentage or to
find some other basis to up the ante with regard to
earthquake resistance.

Buildings designed today under current codes are
only as quake resistant as the current criteria provide, which supposedly reflects the latest thinking
since the 1971 Sylmar quake, the last time a com-
prehensive revision of the code occurred.
Obviously, should there be a quake producing more
devastation than the Sylmar, we will likely have
another upgrade of criteria for typical buildings. It
remains to be seen whether in the aftermath of the
1988 San Francisco earthquake, with its failures on
alluvial soil and collapsing freeways, some major
changes will emerge. From one perspective, it can
be argued that it is really folly for anyone to build in
this earthquake-prone area. Since that includes
most of California, good luck with that notion.

To those who query whether our older designs are
safe, the answer has to be, "Not as safe as if they
were designed today," but that is true of any building built before 1972. In the case of the hillside

platforms above Beverly Glen, for example, it would be feasible to strengthen the support structure substantially even now by adding bracing or gussets to beef-up certain elements. It would be an interesting assignment involving such questions as:

How do you put a dollar value on "some increased resistance," since the result will always fall short of earthquake proof?

How do you value engineer such improvements vs. the effect achieved?

As Art writes, often wind loads govern hillside building design, anyway. However, any buyer would do well to have a competent professional check a building in or before escrow to make sure that proper maintenance has taken place over the years so that the original design is at least viable and functioning.

The book will be most helpful to owners, developers, architects and others who want a detailed overview of the issues which come up in preliminary planning for complex structures whether or not they are in the hills. The approach is the same. Keep all factors in view; decide which determinants to address in what order, keeping feasibility in mind at all times. Remember, the project can get shot down at any point along the way for the most unlikely reasons. It is not at all unheard of for someone to have bought a piece of land on which a permit will not be issued. Why cities don't mark such unbuildable lots on their maps escapes me.

The difficulty in finding out what a building department will accept has been exacerbated in recent years by shrinking city budgets. In Los Angeles, for example, it is now virtually impossible to get an advance reading on what might be the interpretation of a specific code provision. For larger commercial projects you can get an appointment to discuss such questions, but the answers given, like those you get from the IRS hotline, are not binding on the plan checker. This puts the design professional in a very uncomfortable position, one which is hard to explain to an inexperienced client. No solution to this problem is in sight.

Lay people and many developers have the impression that once they have a clear, detailed set of plans approved by the city, they have no further need for the architect or engineer to follow through construction. Any competent contractor can carry them out, right? Wrong. As with the codes, you can get different interpretations of what plan indications mean. The designer may have certain things in mind that can only be communicated if he or she is on site to explain the need for this or that feature.

Furthermore, an owner or developer will sometimes feel that he can take liberties with the plans, going for "equivalent results," not realizing that in making the changes he will be affecting other portions of the job that are seemingly unrelated to the item in question. The design professional, having built the project on paper before putting his ideas into contract documents, may have to explain why a particular change is not in the best interest of the project or its owner.

For example, we created an underfloor space in an older house by rebuilding the foundation. All that separated bedrooms below grade from earth was an 8-inch block wall and the waterproofing had to

be done perfectly, since once subgrade waterproofing fails it is virtually impossible to fix—not to
speak of the horrendous expense and inconve-
nience to the owner. As part of my services, I iden-
tified what I thought was the most conservative
approach, which turned out to be the most expensive. Still, since it was not a large area, the amount of
money involved was relatively small, about $1,000
for the entire waterproofing contract. This was the
lowest of the three bids I obtained from experienced sub-contractors. As part of my research, I
also interviewed the materials manufacturer's repre-
sentative and got him to agree that he would visit
the site with me when installation was starting so
that we could jointly make certain that the work
would proceed correctly.

To my chagrin, the owner informed me that he was
running short of funds and regrettably would not be
able to retain me during construction. Later I found
out that despite my having handed him the bids and
the name of the lowest bidder, he elected to allow
the general contractor to install the waterproofing
himself at what appeared at first to be a savings of
$300 on the contract cost. This,of course, washed
out any chance of getting the manufacturer's rep on
the job, so now we had an inexperienced crew trying to learn on the job how to do this sophisticated
work and no warranty beyond the usual general
contractor's one-year guaranty. I visited the site on
my own and noted with horror that the contractor
had completely misinstalled materials; more, they
were materials which I had not specified.

If the job does leak, even years hence, it will seem
logical "to sue the architect who designed this damn
thing." The cost of professional services during

construction is cheap insurance indeed, considering the complexity of projects these days and the really horrendous consequences of even one major goof undetected during construction. Owners and developers should take serious note of Art's chapter on the team members and their responsibilities.

Art Levin's years of practical experience shine through the pages of this book. I am especially impressed with his attitude of openness and his admonitions for flexibility of approach to solutions for the hillside project. He is the kind of engineer I want on my team.

Dion Neutra, AIA

Preface

Living in the hills attracts people for many reasons: There is more privacy than in the crowded cities or the usual suburbia. The country atmosphere is attractive. The view is often spectacular. Wildlife abounds. There is surrounding vegetation instead of asphalt paving. The attraction is so strong that most hill-dwellers return to the hills even if fire has destroyed their homes.

Although the cost of construction is generally higher in the hills than on level ground, frequently the land is cheaper. If the land is carefully selected and the design and development are intelligently done, high profits can follow.

There are disadvantages to hillside development. Specialized skill is required for both design and construction. Obtaining approval from government authorities can be frustrating, time consuming, and costly. Fire insurance is higher than in the flat lands. Moreover, many people will not live in the hills because of fear of fire or mud slides, transportation problems, or lack of nearby shopping.

Even so, the movement of people into hillside areas continues. Opportunities for hillside development abound and construction in those areas is flourishing

The purpose of this book is to present the owner, architect, structural engineer, and contractor with a knowledgeable approach to hillside building design and development and to introduce him or her to some of the primary advantages, disadvantages, methods, and problems of such buildings. The illustrations are specific aides to solving the problems discussed in the book.

It is not intended here to portray the grandeur of architecture in the hills, nor to impress. Rather, we aim to acquaint the reader with the many approaches to hillside design and construction, to reduce the problems of the architect and builder, to inform the engineer of the variety of structural solutions available to him, and by this process to provide the owner with a better, more economical building.

Frequently, someone asks, "Do I begin with the architect or the structural engineer?" I recommend the following procedure:

1 Select an architect who knows hillside design.

2 Have the architect prepare preliminary sketches.

3 Call in a soils-geology firm to make a preliminary study.

4 Have a surveyor prepare a topographic survey.

5 Choose a structural engineer to recommend changes in the schematic sketches to economize or simplify.

6 Have the soils-geology report completed and, if necessary, submitted to the required authorities for approval.

7 If the soils-geology report is approved, have the architect prepare working drawings to the point where the structural engineer can complete his drawings.

8 In the meantime, have the architect finish his or her design.

Throughout this process, remember that flexible thinking on the part of all involved is essential. Hillside development holds many surprises for the inexperienced—surprises that can have a drastic effect on the cost of construction.

In keeping with the purpose of this as a reference and workbook, the first four chapters deal with factors generic to all hillside development—analyzing and selecting a site, fixing the responsibilities of the individual development team members, determining all possible codes and other restrictions which apply, and listing special survey and geological needs. The remainder of the book is written and organized so that a reader dealing with a particular site configuration, uphill, downhill, or flat, need refer only to those sections dealing with his special problems. Similarly, for ease of use, a number of the drawings are repeated to avoid requiring the reader to leaf back and forth in the book.

1

Site Selection

General Concerns

There are ten factors that affect the selection of the hillside site. A brief discussion of them follows.

1   The view. The view is extremely important. The value of the land and what is built upon it rises with quality of the view. If the view is poor, you might want to reconsider the possible purchase.

2   Steepness of the slope. If the slope is extremely steep (more than 45 degrees) construction is difficult. A person cannot walk easily on such a slope and paths must be cut to provide access. High retaining walls are needed, shoring may be needed for these walls, and costs will increase.

3   General appearance of the neighborhood. If the surrounding area has good-looking homes, is well maintained and well landscaped with flowers and trees, this will increase the value of the proposed project. Contact a real estate agent to determine prevailing sales values.

4   Condition and width of the street. Not only do the appearance and width of the street impress a prospective buyer, but the width affects fire access, and if the street is too narrow it may have to be widened. If the street is paved, check for cracks wide enough to indicate earth movement in the downhill direction.

5   Availability of utilities. Generally in developed areas electricity, gas, and water are available.

•   Electricity. The power company will usually provide lines to the proposed building and the electrician can then extend the lines from the above roof head to the main service panel. Where electricity is not available, a motor generator or, more rarely, a turbine generator can be used. Easements for electric lines also affect hillside development. An easement can exist without being recorded, which means that when you see electric lines over a proposed property, you should realize that unless you pay to have them relocated, they will be an easement limiting the development. There are requirements for distances away from the lines both horizontally and vertically. If it is necessary to install underground electric service the cost of a development will of course go up. This possibility should be thoroughly checked out. If above-ground lines cross the front of the property, the result is the same as a required front setback.

- Gas. The gas company will usually place a meter at a reasonable distance from the street, and a plumber can then install piping from the meter to the building. If gas is not available, propane frequently can be used.

- Water. The water company will place its meter in the public way. A plumber can then extend water lines to a pressure regulator and to all desired facilities. If municipal water is not available, a well is usually drilled. To find an approximate cost for a well, check with some drilling companies in the vicinity.

- Sewerage

Sewer. If there is no sewer at the property involved, the cost of bringing up a main line sewer can be substantial. If the proposed building is to have a floor below street level, check the required depth of the line at the building area. It might be necessary to install a sump pump. Or look into the possibility and feasibility of carrying sewage through an easement to a street below.

Seepage pit and septic tank. Sometimes a seepage pit must be constructed and tested before a building permit is issued. If the earth cannot absorb the effluent, and the test fails, the land has little value. The soils-geology report should address this problem. For a narrow lot, the location of the septic tank, seepage pit, and future seepage pit (a standard requirement in case the first pit later fails) must be carefully planned. For example, to provide the required clearances among these units as well as from side lines and from the dwelling it is sometimes necessary to move the building away from the street. Other systems are sometimes required. Check with the authorities for these.

6   Legal requirements of jurisdiction involved. Many requirements pertain to both zoning and building, and the architect should check their effects upon the proposed development. Some of these requirements should be determined before making an offer for the property. (See chapter 3 for legal requirements.)

7   Soil and geology. If many properties are being investigated, as they often are, the owner and architect should observe the terrain and try to imagine the natural slope of the ground before any man-made fill might have been placed on it. It is frequently possible to determine roughly how much fill there is. Before buying hillside property, I strongly recommend that you engage a soils-geology firm to make a preliminary study that includes visual inspection, examination of all available existing documentation, and, if necessary, some underground exploration to determine the approximate depths of fill and geologic hazards. Is the property in a landslide area? Is there a record of earthquake faults?

If the lot is to have a seepage pit, the study should also include a statement of whether such a pit can be satisfactorily installed. (See chapter 5 on soil and geology.)

8 Location of the front property line. The location of the front property line is important because the height of retaining walls and the ease of access to the required parking area are affected. The approximate location of this line can sometimes be found from the centerline of an existing paved street as shown on local jurisdiction maps. On occasion, the developed properties along a street give some indication. Otherwise, a survey may have to be made.

9 Size and shape of the lot. The size and shape of the lot can have considerable effect upon a proposed building. For example, the size may not meet the minimum requirements of the local jurisdiction, and the shape may dictate the location of the building.

10 Covenants, conditions, and restrictions (CC&Rs). Although CC&Rs influence all properties, they can seriously affect hillside properties.

• A front easement generally means higher retaining walls and, for a downhill site, a higher building.

In one of my projects, an uphill site had a front setback requirement of 25 feet. We moved the building uphill, and constructed a long driveway with retaining walls along the uphill face. Fortunately, the lot was wide, and the property was valuable enough to permit the extra costs. This is not always the case.

• An easement through a lot but not near a side line can mean moving a proposed building to an undesirable location.

In another of my projects, an easement for sewerage and drainage was found to exist where a building was to be constructed, which required the foundation system to span the easement.

- An easement for sewer and drainage purposes on an adjacent property below a proposed site can be used to advantage. For example, a sewer in the street of the proposed building may not be accessible to a lower level bath unless a sump pump is installed, whereas sewage lines could be carried down through the easement along with roof, deck, and pad drainage. Although a sump pump can be used for sewage, it is not usually practical for drainage. If there is a storm and electricity fails, the pump will not work, and a secondary source of power, such as a motor generator, is rarely installed—sometimes because of cost and, often, because the architect did not think of it.

- Providing a new easement across one lot for access to a second lot is a reasonable way to develop two or three properties simultaneously. Where this method is used for a third property, the authorities sometimes require that a private street be built which entails complying with additional legal requirements.

- Some hill properties are so irregularly shaped that a portion of one lot may have little value to that lot but may have great value to a second, adjacent property. Many zoning ordinances will not allow the sale of this portion (the remaining area might fall below the minimum lot size), but the granting of an easement to the second property could achieve the same objective.

The Downhill Site

The downhill lot is on the downhill side of a street. Some of the advantages of such a lot are the following:

- Buildings here are easier to construct than those on an uphill site because building materials are carried down rather than up.

- The view is generally better and not blocked by another building.

- There is generally less need for grading, shoring, and retaining walls.

  Some disadvantages are these:

- Many persons are afraid of heights; they are terrified of walking toward the view wall or standing on a cantilevered deck high above a ground surface that drops away at a steep angle. The sloping ground below accentuates the height more than does the street of an uphill building.

- A closely related disadvantage is that the downhill-site building appears less secure than the uphill building, particularly if the underfloor space is not enclosed.

- The foundation system is more complicated than that used for an uphill building.

The Uphill Site

The uphill lot is one that is on the uphill side of the street. Grading and retaining walls are usually required. Some advantages of the uphill site are:

- Buildings on an uphill sites are more saleable than those on downhill sites. The fear-of-heights problem can be greatly reduced by careful architectural design, and a generally more secure feeling can be achieved than for the downhill building.

- It is easy to provide pleasant patio facilities in the cleared space generally required behind (uphill from) the building.

Some disadvantages are these:

- High retaining walls and shoring are frequently required, and costs can increase dramatically.

- Earth slides (particularly after a fire has denuded the hill above) and rock slides can damage or destroy a building, possibly resulting in lawsuits against the owner, architect, engineer, and contractor. Proper design and construction can reduce the possibility of slides.

- Some authorities require regrading a steep slope adjacent to a street to a maximum angle of 45 degrees. This can be an unexpected cost.

- If the required grading is high above the street level, the authorities may also require you to install many drainage devices, another unexpected cost.

The Flat or Terraced Hillside Site

The flat or terraced hillside lot is generally the result of either cutting or filling a property (or both) to make it level. Do not assume that a level site at a bend in, or at the end of, a street is all natural soil. It frequently consists of fill that was deposited when the street was constructed.

Some advantages of such a lot are the following:

- Where the lot has been cut and the soil is natural (not fill), the footings can be the same as on a non-hillside flat property and are economical and easy

to construct. Engineering the foundation is not generally required.

- It is easy to store building materials on the property
  and easy to get them to the construction area.

- Providing access to the parking area is usually
  simple.

- Landscaping the area is easy.

- Drainage is generally not difficult to install: the pad
  is merely sloped to drain.

  Some disadvantages are these:

- The cost of flat or terraced land is usually
  considerable.

- If the soil is compacted fill that has been placed
  properly (see chapter 5) then standard footings can
  be used. If the soil is not compacted, however, footings must extend through the fill into proper bearing
  soil or rock below. Costs can increase substantially.

- If the soil consists of both fill and natural materials,
  a special problem arises. If standard footings are
  used, the building will likely suffer major damage
  from differential settlement. To prevent this, one of
  three things must be done: deepen the footings (if
  the fill depth is small), penetrate the fill with a more
  complicated foundation system, or regrade the site
  to provide compacted fill throughout.

2

Professional Team

2

A team of six professionals is generally needed for a well-planned building project: architect, surveyor, soils-geology consultant, structural engineer, civil engineer, and landscape architect. These six and their functions and responsibilities are described in this section.

Architect

The architect is the overall planner and organizer for the development. His responsibilities can include the following.

On-Site Check

First, if possible, the architect should assist the client in selecting the building site. At the property he should check:

- The view. How should the building be oriented for maximum advantage?

- The steepness of the slope. Too steep? Where should the building be placed?

- The general appearance of the neighborhood.

- Condition and width of the street. Large cracks? If so, there could be a soils or geology problem.

- The availability of utilities.

- The location of neighboring buildings. Will they have any effect on:

Retaining walls?

The view from windows?

Automobile access?

Building entry or egress?

- For possible drainage problems.

- The location of existing poles, hydrants, and other obstacles.

- With the soils-geology consultant. If either of them sees any possible soil problems, then the consultant should make a preliminary study. The study could include, if necessary, test pits or borings, but a full report is not essential at this point.

Legal Check

Next, after observing the site, the architect should check all legal requirements (see chapter 3) including CC&Rs.

Record Check of Utilities

The architect must examine records for available utilities, especially sewerage facilities.

Escrow Recommendations

If all items checked out favor the financial feasibility of the project, and the owner is satisfied, the architect should recommend that an escrow be opened. I strongly urge including in the escrow a provision that the property purchase be contingent upon the approval of the soils-geology report by the structural engineer. It is not sufficient for the contingency to depend on the authorities' approval of the report because they might approve but require considerable grading or other costly measures to stabilize the site.

Preliminary Sketches

At this point, the architect should make a preliminary outline of the building, showing its location on the property.

Engaging a Surveyor

The architect should then engage a surveyor to prepare a topographic survey and to place corner monuments.

Coordinating with the Structural Engineer

With topographic survey and preliminary soils-geology report in hand, the architect should discuss the proposed layout with the structural engineer to determine if it creates any structural problems or unnecessary foundation costs.

Coordinating with the Soils-Geology Consultant

The architect should consult with the soils-geology consultants and have them prepare a final report that he can use to determine:

- The stability of the site.

- The location of maximum fill.

- The maximum angle of cuts and fills.

- Any earthquake faults or landslide conditions.

- Any sewerage requirements if no sewer exists.

- Any requirements for existing nonconforming slopes.

- The clearance requirements from steep slopes.

- If there is a high water table problem.

- The possibility of finding gases during excavation.

If necessary, the soils-geology report is submitted to the authorities for approval. If it is approved, the architect again consults with the structural engineer, and the design phase then begins.

Coordinating the Design

The architect provides the architectural planning, design, drawings, and specifications, and coordinates the activities of the structural engineer, civil engineer, and landscape architect during these preparations.

Obtaining Permits and Variances

At this point the architect processes the plans and reports through the local jurisdiction to obtain the necessary permits and variances.

Contract Administration

Last, the architect handles all contract administration, including:

- Obtaining bids from building contractors.

- Observing construction.

- Authorizing payments to the builder after checking for lien releases.

- Filing a notice of completion.

Surveyor

The surveyor is responsible for:

- Setting permanent property corner monuments. A stake with a ribbon attached is not sufficient. Antagonistic neighbors have been known to move these.

- Providing a topographic map (see chapter 4).

- Providing grade stakes where grading is required.

- Staking the location of the foundation and retaining walls.

post grading survey ✳

- Rechecking the topography after any grading is completed.

Soils-Geology Consultant

The soils-geology consultant may be one person or a large firm whose responsibilities include the following:

Preliminary Assessment

The soils-geology consultant makes a preliminary assessment of the property to help the prospective owner decide whether to purchase. He also tentatively determines the stability of the site.

Test Borings

The soils-geology consultant next has test borings made to determine:

- Depths of fill and topsoil.
- Type of soil or rock below.
- Water level.
- Geologic structure and hazards.
- Existence of gases.

Making Recommendations

The soils-geology consultant makes recommendations concerning the following:

- Drainage.
- Shoring.
- Foundation design.
- Grading.
- Sewerage if no sewer exists.

Soil Testing and Geologic Planning

Here the consultant has the soil laboratory-tested. Following this, he or she provides a geologic plan showing cross sections through the property and determines the stability of the site.

Preparing a Report

Next the soils-geology consultant prepares a report including all the above-mentioned findings and recommendations.

Testing New Man-made Fill

Another responsibility of the soils engineer is to make tests of new man-made fill to determine if the compaction meets the specifications.

Structural Engineer

The structural engineer's responsibilities include the following:

Structural Plans

The structural engineer provides the design and plans for rafters, beams, floor joists, the foundations, and retaining walls, and—for earthquake resistance—straps, bolts, and plywood for roof, floors, and walls. The foundation and retaining walls are costly to construct. Finding an engineer who knows hillside design is essential.

Wind and Seismic Design

Before the structural design, the owner should decide whether the structural engineer should provide for only the minimum materials required by the building codes, or whether, in localities subject to seismic or heavy wind forces, the engineer should

greater than
minimum
design *

provide for a stronger-than-minimum structure. The cost of these additional materials is not significant, but the design is more time consuming and therefore more costly.

Civil Engineer

grading
sewer ✳

A civil engineer is required when there is need for design of subdivisions, grading, streets, sewer, or drainage facilities. Minor drainage design is usually by the architect.

Landscape Architect

The landscape architect is sometimes required by state law, and can be helpful when there is to be a large amount of landscaping or when specialized design is desired. In addition to specifying plants and trees, plans should include irrigation, small walls, and drainage.

Codes and Other Restrictions

3

Zoning Requirements

Zoning regulations vary among jurisdictions. So great are these differences for hillside areas that it is imperative to verify major requirements before purchasing property and proceeding with the design. Some communities, in attempting to slow growth, are passing legislation that creates moratoriums in certain hill areas. In addition, specific plans sometimes replace general plans. These ordinances either prohibit construction or require items not necessary elsewhere.

specific plans vs general plan

If possible, plan the development so that variances are not needed. Variances frequently include special demands regarding building appearance, fences, roofing, and so forth.

Check zoning codes for the following:

1 Setbacks from all property lines.

2 Allowable number of stories.

3 Quantity and size of parking spaces. Must these spaces be in a garage or a carport? Is tandem parking permitted?

4 Width of the driveway and paving.

5 Street frontage. If the lot does not have frontage, is it permitted to build there?

6 Legality of the lot. Is the property just a portion of a lot? If so, it may not be a legal lot. Occasionally, an owner, not knowing this, sells a part of a lot to a neighbor.

7 Allowable minimum size. If the lot is below the allowable minimum, it does not necessarily mean that there will be a problem in obtaining a permit.

Some properties were subdivided before a zoning ordinance was passed, and construction is permitted.

8 Allowable maximum building height. The maximum height limitation could make design difficult. The maximum allowable residential building heights in the Los Angeles area, for example, can vary from 30 to 57 feet. (The height is measured from a point five feet away from the lowest point of the building to the top of the building at its highest point.) The most convenient limitation I have found (at the time of writing) is in Laguna Beach, California, where official literature shows a profile within which construction must take place. In general, the top of construction must be within 30 feet of the grade immediately below.

9 Allowable projections into required yards.

10 Allowable additional buildings. If the owner wants the project to consist of more than one building, is that permitted? How far apart must the buildings be? Are the contemplated uses of the additional buildings permitted?

Building Requirements

Check the following building requirements:

1 Maximum building height for the type of construction intended. Usually, a wood frame structure is not permitted to be as high as a concrete structure. In the hills, however, the zoning height limitation usually governs.

2 Number of exits and the distance between them. How many exits are required? How is the distance between them measured? If a center stairway is contemplated, a required second stairway can be

difficult to place. May it be in a required yard?

3 Automatic fire-sprinkler system. Is one required?

4 Horizontal distance between a bedroom and ground. Where the ground height is well above that of the floor, the bedroom may be called a cellar, and sleeping in a cellar is frequently not permitted.

5 Insulation and maximum allowable glass area.

6 Roof material. Must the roof be of a specific material?

7 Smoke alarms.

8 Security systems.

9 Handicapped access and facilities.

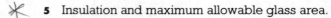

10 Special wind force provisions. (Check with the structural engineer.) If any windows are larger than usual, the glass should be correspondingly thicker. In one house I had structurally designed, during a violent storm the wind blew a large window pane inward. The shattered glass showered onto a bed that the owners had—fortunately—left only a short time before. The architect had not discussed glass type or thickness with me during design. Tempered glass is required by some jurisdictions.

11 Any special approvals or variances.

12 One-hour fire-resistive construction.

13 Stairways. For example, may a spiral stairway be used?

14 Building code. Which one is used?

Grading Requirements

 1 Existing nonconforming cuts or fills. Are there any special requirements for these? Sometimes they must be made to conform.

 2 Soils-geology report. Does it have to be approved? If it does, it should be submitted before proceeding with the building design.

3 Landslide areas and earthquake faults. Is the property in a landslide area? Is there a record of earthquake faults? These questions should have been asked and answered during the site selection process as part of the considerations for purchase. They now affect site treatment.

4 Distance from a steep slope. Must the building be a specific distance from a steep slope, either ascending or descending? The answer can drastically affect both design and cost.

5 Maximum allowable angle for proposed cuts or fills.

6 Grading next to the public way or other property lines. Are there any special requirements?

7 Special hazards.

 8 Drainage. On a downhill site with no street below, delivering drainage to a street would require an easement below or a special disbursing device.

9 Allowable shoring systems.

Miscellaneous Requirements

1 Approval of an art jury. Is such an approval necessary? What are its requirements?

2 Tree removal. Is there a restriction against removing trees?

3 Required and existing easements. Also, are there any existing easements on adjacent properties?

4 Location and depth of sewer. If there is no sewer, what allowable sewerage systems are permitted, and what are their requirements? For a seepage pit and septic tank, check the locations of and the separations between them and any buildings as well as the required depth for the pit.

5 The public way. What work is necessary in the public way, and what are the specific requirements? Street design by a civil engineer may be necessary.

6 Highways. Is the property on a major or secondary highway? If so, the owner may have to give a small part of the it to the local municipality. For example, the city of Los Angeles requires an owner to donate a strip of property along the street frontage to permit street widening. This must be done before a building permit is issued, and the procedure is time consuming.

4

Survey and Topography

4

The usual reasons for surveying a site, including installing property corner monuments and locating easements, also apply, of course, to hillside properties. However, the requirement for properly placing the proposed structure is more important for hillside property than for flat land. It is not easy to locate proposed footings or retaining walls where the land slopes steeply, and if such land is covered with brush, plants, and trees, it is difficult to obtain an accurate topographic survey. Yet such a survey is essential for hillside properties.

Corner Monuments

It is important to have corner monuments marking the front property line. If this line is some distance from the street, retaining walls must be higher, and on a downhill site the architect can find it difficult to keep the building height within the maximum allowable limits.

Building Location

Before the survey begins, the architect should show the surveyor the approximate building location. This information will help the surveyor to prepare a good topographic plan. If the building location is not known, the contours (see Topographic Plan, following) will have to be placed at much closer intervals than would otherwise be required.

Topographic Plan

The topographic plan should show contours at 5-foot elevation changes except in the area of the proposed building where 2-foot changes should be shown. Such contours are for a single building. Where development includes numerous buildings on a large property, the overall plan should show contours at anywhere from 10- to 50-foot intervals. Each building site would then have its own plan showing contours at the 2- and 5-foot variations.

The topographic plan should include not only the property to be developed but also the street on the opposite side of the building site and should extend approximately 10 feet into adjacent properties. Changes in elevation from one site to an adjoining site can vary considerably, and design of retaining walls, drainage devices, excavations, grading, shoring, and so on, can be affected. Also, fences, retaining walls, and buildings on adjacent properties can create surcharged loads that affect retaining wall designs.

surcharged loads

survey before soils

The topographic survey should be prepared before the soils-geology report is made because it is necessary for the preparation of cross sections through the property that the soils-geology report should include.

Footing and Retaining Wall Locations

I recommend that all footings, including retaining wall footings, be located by the surveyor. If these structural elements are incorrectly located, it may force redesign of portions of the foundation. Since construction often obliterates the surveyor's stakes, these markers should be located far enough away from the building to protect them during construction.

Grade Stakes and Topography Recheck

Where there is to be grading, grade stakes are used to show proposed grade elevations. After grading is finished, it is strongly recommended that the new topography be shown on a plan. The proposed elevations on the original plan may not be the elevations after grading. Also check the new grades with the design to determine if any revisions are necessary.

5

Soils and Geology

5

The soil and geology of hillside land are of vital importance to the prospective purchaser. Some sites are unbuildable; others are buildable only at great expense. For example, a site can be unbuildable in a landslide area. Although a site may be buildable on or near an earthquake fault, it should certainly not be built upon unaware. Shale or slate with their bedding planes sloping toward the proposed construction can require retaining walls designed for heavier than normal pressures and may require shoring for the wall excavation. Massive amounts of man-made fill may overlie the natural soil or rock below. Such fill is usually found on downhill sites, having been deposited there when the street above was constructed. At a dead-end street, or at a bend in a street, a level lot may appear to be of natural soil when actually it could have a great deal of fill from the excavated street. On an uphill site, fill may be at the front of a lot if the street itself is on fill.

After the owner and architect inspect a prospective site and believe it to be acceptable, the soils-geology firm should make a preliminary investigation. This may be just a visual inspection, or it may include subsurface exploration, but an opinion at this time—and a preliminary report—is of considerable importance.

The Report

The following eleven items should be covered in the soils-geology final report:

1 A statement concerning the stability of the site. Although a piece of land may have existed for centuries without sliding downhill, there is no guarantee that there will be no slide after a building is

stability analysis

constructed upon it. A stability analysis should disclose such a possibility.

At one site a dwelling was constructed with a foundation system consisting of caissons and grade beams. Underground springs produced enough water to fracture the rock beneath the caissons. The mass of rock above the fracture and the building began moving downhill at a rate of about $1/4$ inch per hour. Within a few hours I had designed two large buttresses of reinforced concrete that were constructed at the lower end of the rock fracture and movement of the building and the fractured rock was halted. The next day, under the supervision of soils engineer G.S. Kovacs, pipes were installed to relieve the underground water pressure. (A county inspector, seeing the buttress construction in progress, demanded that work be stopped and a permit obtained even though his office was closed for the day! His demand was ignored. By the next morning the building would have been at the bottom of the hill.)

2 Subsurface exploration results. This part of the report should include the following information:

- Types of soil.

- Depth of man-made fill.

- Depth of top soil.

- Water table. If water is found, it can hinder construction, but it is possible for foundations to be in water.

- Any geologic hazards (if found).

- Logs of test pits or boring results.

- Presence of gases (if found).

Figure 1

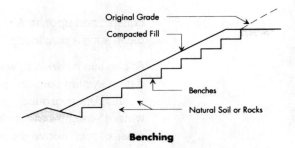

Benching

Figure 2

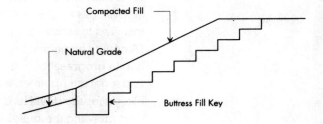

3 Engineering parameters for the design of retaining walls and footings.

4 Grading. Recommendations for the following information should be included:

- Maximum angles of slopes for cuts and fills.

- Maximum allowable height of a cut without providing for shoring.

- Sections cut through the property showing fill and topsoil, and the angles of any slate or shale.

- Drainage recommendations for both the surface and the subsurface.

- Benching recommendations. Where new compacted fill is to be placed on a sloping site, level steps must be cut in the existing soil or rock before compacting (fig. 1).

  Many houses in the Santa Monica Mountains in Southern California were built on compacted fill that had been placed without following such a procedure, and eventually the fill slipped downhill. This slippage caused substantial damage to both dwellings and swimming pools.

- Buttress fill recommendations. A buttress fill is a hill of compacted fill constructed at the lower portion of an unstable slope and benched into solid natural material at the bottom (fig. 2).

- Shoring recommendations, including the soil pressure against the shoring.

- Recommendations for grading during the rainy season. If possible, grading should be avoided during heavy rainy seasons because of the possibility of mud slides. Also, heavy equipment can bog

Figure 3

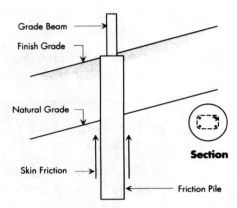

Grade Beam

Finish Grade

Natural Grade

Section

Skin Friction

Friction Pile

Figure 4

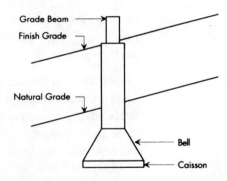

Grade Beam

Finish Grade

Natural Grade

Bell

Caisson

Figure 5

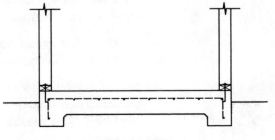

Floating Slab

down. When large quantities of earth are exported
from the building site, political problems can arise:
large trucks moving in residential areas cause
noise, dust (during dry seasons), and vibration.
Complaints to the authorities are not uncommon.
Watering down dust and cautioning and supervising
the truck drivers help alleviate the problem.

- Compaction requirements.

- Any special precautions. Two examples might be
  methods of preventing water from draining onto a
  slope and causing mud slides, and recommending
  the provision of a fence at the bottom of a lot to prevent damage to an adjacent property.

5 Recommendations for the method of support of
buildings and structures. This part of the report
should include information about the following:

- Friction piles. These are cast-in-place, reinforced
  concrete columns that are drilled or dug through fill
  and topsoil into natural materials to a depth
  sufficient to provide enough friction around the column to support the loads on the pile (fig. 3).

- Belled caissons. These are cast-in-place, reinforced
  concrete columns that have spread-type footings
  (called bells) at the bottom (fig. 4).

- Retaining wall design.

- Floating slabs (for a flat lot). These are reinforced
  concrete slabs used to spread the load of the building over the area of the foundation (fig. 5).

- Special footings (for a flat lot or expansive soil).
  Usually these footings have a little more depth than
  standard footings and a little more reinforcing steel.

Figure 6

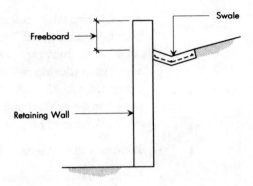

Figure 7

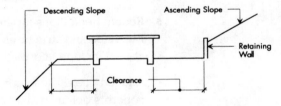

- Buildings to be constructed on flat land that consists of both fill and natural materials. If ordinary footings are used, which rest on both types of soil, differential settlement could destroy the building. Proper design would have the building supported on compacted fill only, or on deepened footings that extend into only natural soil. Piles or caissons can also be used.

- The height of retaining wall freeboard. Freeboard is the portion of a retaining wall that extends above the higher grade and that prevents earth or rock slides from going over the wall (fig. 6).

- Creep force against caissons or piles. Man-made fill on a slope has a tendency, over time, to slide downhill. The force of the fill against piles or caissons is called a creep force.

- Footing clearance from a descending slope (fig. 7).

6 Clearance of buildings or structures from ascending slopes (fig. 7).

7 Anticipated settlement of the foundation.

8 Results of laboratory testing of the natural soil.

9 Recommendations for waterproofing rooms below grade.

10 Recommendations for drainage of roof, slopes, and pads.

11 Recommendations for sewerage where no sewer exists.

Approval of Report

Some jurisdictions require that the soils-geology report be approved before they will issue a building permit. Where this is necessary, it is recommended that no working drawings or structural design begin before the report is submitted; denial of the report would make these efforts useless. Also, the authorities may have additional requirements that will affect the designs.

Observation of Construction

The soils-geology firm should be engaged to inspect excavations, grading (including making compaction tests), and shoring to ensure that the recommendations of their report are followed. In particular, they should confirm the depth of penetration of a pile, caisson, or footing into the recommended material. The firm should also confirm the direction of the rock planes where there is shale or slate. If the direction is different from that given in the original report, it can affect the stability of the building and could require shoring.

Grading and Plants

Downhill Sites

Grading of downhill sites is best avoided. However, some jurisdictions require fill to be at a maximum slope of 26 degrees (one vertical to two horizontal), and if existing fill is at a slope steeper than this, grading and perhaps retaining walls will be necessary. Investigate the possibility of this need carefully because of the cost and time required for such work.

Uphill Sites

Uphill sites have special needs for the protection of proposed buildings. Current building codes generally require a clearance from a building to the rear ascending slope. To comply, retaining walls are usually constructed behind and parallel to the building. Unfortunately, this clearance and wall are often insufficient to prevent mud slides from going over the wall and damaging the structure. A far safer and less costly procedure is to construct a retaining wall (with a freeboard) behind the building that in plan view is in the form of an inverted V with the point of the V extending uphill (fig. 8). Such a wall diverts earth, rock, or mud around the building. In some jurisdictions this method requires special approval.

Grading uphill sites for the garage and the rear area clearance discussed above is generally expected. However, at times grading is also required to reduce the angle of a slope adjacent to a street to 45 degrees.

If the height of a retaining wall can be reduced by grading, it is usually economical to do so. The most likely area for this grading is under a building (fig. 9).

Terracing

Cutting terraced lots on shallow slope properties is highly recommended. Many of the problems associated with steep slopes are avoided, and the development is more attractive and saleable (fig. 10).

Shoring

Shoring is required (1) where slopes to be cut are unstable, (2) where an excavation is near an

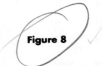

Figure 8

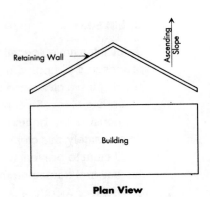

Retaining Wall

Ascending Slope

Building

Plan View

Figure 9

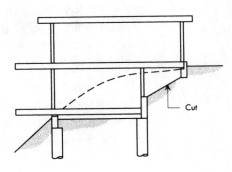

Cut

Figure 10

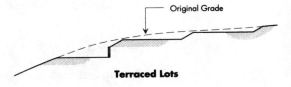

Original Grade

Terraced Lots

Figure 11

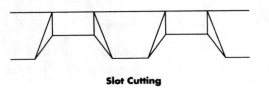

Slot Cutting

existing structure, or (3) where grading would undermine an existing street that must remain in use with its full width undisturbed. Unstable slopes are those composed of soils with loose sand or that have rocks, such as shale, with planes slanting downward toward a proposed structure. Shoring near an existing structure frequently requires underpinning the existing building as well as shoring the vertical banks of the excavation. Sometimes slot-cutting (excavating a part of the area, building a part of the retaining wall, then repeating the process) is used but this is time consuming and costly (fig. 11).

grade beam-pile
retaining wall
- tie-back system

When a grade beam-pile retaining wall is used (see chapter 7), shoring can be incorporated into its construction. Otherwise, shoring consists of steel, wood, or poured-in-place concrete piles. Tie-back systems of various kinds are also used when vehicle access is possible.

Planting

After slopes are graded, they should be planted and an automatic sprinkler system installed. The plant roots eventually help prevent erosion, and, of course, plants improve the appearance of the site, making it more saleable. Not all plants are acceptable, however. For example, the city of Los Angeles maintains a list of permitted grasses, shrubs, and trees. When there is no such list available, follow the advice of a landscape architect or other specialist.

6

Architectural

6

Piles, Caissons, Grade Beams

All buildings on downhill lots, and some buildings on uphill and hillside flat or terraced lots, must have friction piles or belled caissons supporting grade beams, which means that architects must be very familiar with these, structural members. They do not need to know how to structurally design them, but they should certainly know what they are and how they are used.

A poured-in-place friction pile is a reinforced concrete column constructed by first drilling or hand-digging a hole deep enough through man-made fill and topsoil into natural materials to provide enough friction around the column to support the loads imposed (figs. 13 and 14). Then reinforcing steel is placed, and the concrete is poured. The friction piles are usually used to support grade beams. Sometimes they are used as shoring.

A belled caisson is similar to a pile in construction and use. It too is cast in place, but it is not embedded as deeply into the natural material as a pile (fig. 15). It has a spread-type footing (shaped like a bell) at the bottom, and this bell distributes its load in same manner as a standard footing.

The choice of piles or caissons is usually determined by the underlying, supporting soil. If it is a dense rock such as basalt, penetrating it with a friction pile may not be possible. However, in most cases, the pile is the better choice.

A grade beam is a reinforced concrete beam that has its bottom resting on the finish grade. It should be embedded 12" to 18" to prevent erosion of the soil around the building. Such erosion may leave spaces under the grade beam. Animals often use these spaces to access the area under the building. Grade beams are supported by piles, caissons, or even by spread footings, and they are used to support buildings.

Figure 13

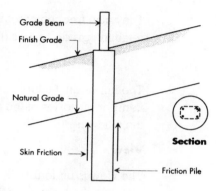

Grade Beam

Finish Grade

Natural Grade

Skin Friction

Friction Pile

Section

Figure 14

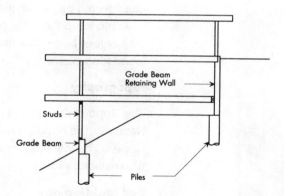

Grade Beam
Retaining Wall

Studs

Grade Beam

Piles

Figure 15

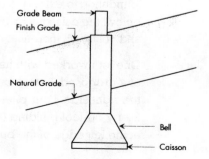

Grade Beam

Finish Grade

Natural Grade

Bell

Caisson

They also frequently retain earth, and are then retaining grade beams (fig. 16).

The Downhill Building

The important factors affecting the location and the number of stories of the downhill building include the following:

View

The view is undoubtedly the most important factor affecting the location of the building and the placement of the important rooms (living, dining, and bedrooms), the decks, and the windows. Also, in considering the orientation of the building, when possible keep the walls parallel to the street along the contour lines. This makes construction of the foundation easier.

Topography

The slope of the ground may vary considerably. Naturally, the building should be placed where the slope is shallow unless the view or fill depth is unsatisfactory there.

Soil and Geology

 The building should be placed where grading and the depth of fill are at a minimum. Otherwise, for the foundation to extend to the desirable soil or rock below, the caissons or piles will have to be longer and costs will increase.

One lot I worked with had 4 feet of fill at the left side of a proposed 3-story building and 24 feet of fill at the right side. Four piles were used to construct the 30-by-50-foot building (fig. 17). Two of these were at the left edge of the building; the other two were

Figure 16

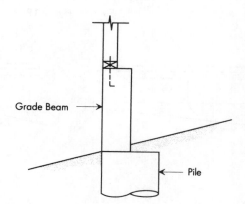

Grade Beam

Pile

Figure 17

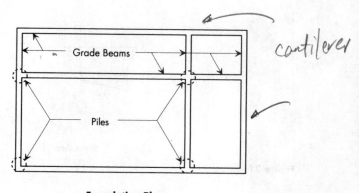

Grade Beams

Piles

cantilever

Foundation Plan

Figure 18

Figure 19

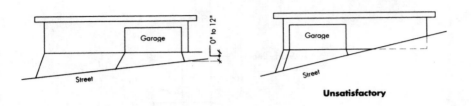

Unsatisfactory

Figure 20

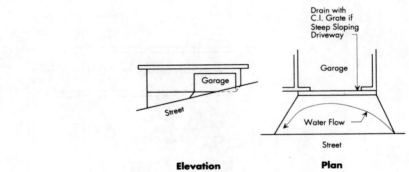

Elevation

Plan

Figure 21

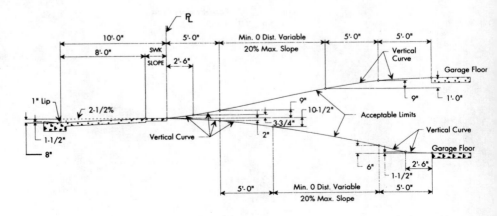

35 feet to the right. The building thus cantilevered 15 feet toward the right and 10 feet to the rear. This placement of the building avoided the deepest part of the fill; and that, along with keeping the number of piles to four, resulted in reasonable foundation costs.

Garage Access

On a sloping street, the garage or carport should be placed at the highest elevation of the lot next to the street (fig. 18). It is generally best to have the garage floor and the dwelling floor leading to it at the same elevation; if you were instead to put the garage at the lower elevation along the street (fig. 19), a portion of the house would be below street level and would require retaining walls. This could also cause drainage problems in the area between the dwelling and the street.

If the street is so narrow that a 90-degree turn from it into the driveway is not possible, then the garage must be turned at an angle to the street, be set back from the street, or have a wide driveway. When possible, to avoid water from the street running into the garage, make the garage floor at least 12 inches above the street at the high side of the driveway.

When the street slopes steeply, the garage floor should be at least at the same elevation (higher if possible) as the street opposite the center of the driveway (fig. 20), otherwise parts of the driveway will be too steep. Alternatively, you might set the garage farther back from the street. It is not desirable to have a two-level garage. Not only can cars be damaged, but people can easily miss the step and fall.

The slope of a good driveway should conform to the slopes shown in figure 21. In climates where ice can form, these slopes must be less. Concrete driveway paving should have a broom finish.

Only where the property is very valuable should a long driveway down a steep hillside be considered: the cost of the retaining walls would be prohibitive. The width of a long driveway, where cars going in opposite directions may have to pass, should be 18 to 20 feet. The minimum width for a one-direction driveway is 10 to 12 feet. These widths depend partly on the sharpness of any required curves. Placing the garage as close to the street as possible is, of course, the least expensive.

Where a garage floor is to consist of $3^1/2$ inches of concrete over felt over plywood over wood joists, the concrete should have as little water content when poured as possible and still be handled. (There should be full shower pan construction if a room is to be below.) In addition, to reduce concrete cracking, cold joints should be used.

A tire stop should be provided to prevent a vehicle from accidentally continuing downhill.

Location of the Front Property Line

The location of the front property line can create special problems:

If the line is close to the street and the street is narrow, constructing a floor one level down and close to the line means that a retaining wall at least 11 feet high will be needed at the front of the building (fig. 22), and that can mean shoring the street.

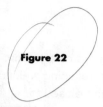

Figure 22

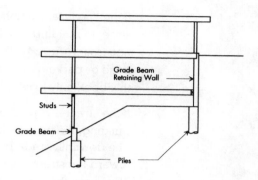

Figure 23

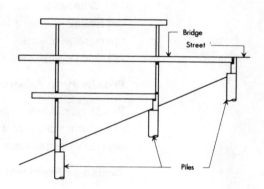

Figure 24

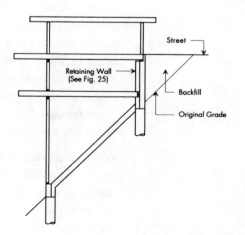

If the line is far from the street, either a bridge from
street to building (fig. 23) or a high retaining wall is
necessary (fig. 24). The bridge can be used for a
patio or parking. (Flat roofs are shown throughout
this book only to simplify the illustrations.)

- If the street is only about 10 or 12 feet from the
building, the piles at the street can be eliminated.
The downhill grade beams can just cantilever
toward the street to pick up the beam at the street.
(This uses the same principle as shown in figure
26.) Where the front line is far from the street, building height can be a large problem. Two buildings,
the garage at street level and the dwelling down the
hill, is a possible solution (fig. 27).

Proximity to Adjacent Buildings

Buildings close to a proposed building can affect the
view from windows, retaining wall heights, and
entries or egresses.

Drainage Problems

Drainage for the downhill building site is not usually
as difficult as for the uphill site. Water from the roof,
from decks that do not have spaced decking, from
the driveway, and from any graded or paved area
should be delivered to a street, drainage canal, or
natural watercourse using gutters, downspouts, and
other nonerosive devices (such as pipes or concrete swales). Drainage into a sewerage system is
generally not approved.

Where it is not possible to deliver water to any of
these acceptable locations, a disbursement system
can be designed to change concentrated flow to
almost a sheet flow by conducting the water to a
horizontal concrete or masonry wall that has many

Figure 25

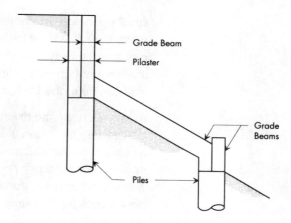

Grade Beam

Pilaster

Grade
Beams

Piles

Figure 26

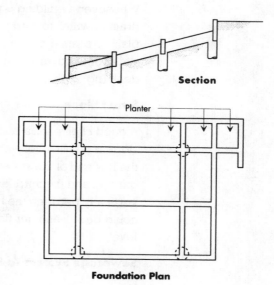

Section

Planter

Foundation Plan

small openings. To prevent the wall from washing down the hill, it must be supported by a grade beam and pile system (fig. 28) unless the slope is shallow enough so that an ordinary small retaining wall can be embedded in natural soil.

At one such site the drainage wall was supported by the existing fill. When the fill was washed out during a rain storm, the wall also was washed out. At another site a sump pump was used to discharge the water into the street above. When a storm caused a power outage, the pump failed and a mud slide occurred.

Whenever a building is placed so that water can drain downhill toward it, it is important either to plan for drainage to protect the building from mud slides or to cover the area with an impervious deck (fig. 29).

Street Slope

A good choice for a building on a street with a steep slope is a split level with the garage on one level at the low end of the street, a second level above the garage, and the third level to the side and halfway vertically between the two (figs. 30 and 31). There could be still another floor under this third middle level.

Sewerage System To Be Used

Where a main line sewer is available, it is used, of course. When another system is necessary, contact the authorities to determine specific requirements. Restrictions concerning distances between a seepage pit, septic tank, and building can affect the building location. Also, providing for a possible future seepage pit is sometimes required.

Figure 27

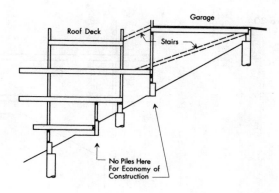

Garage

Roof Deck

Stairs

No Piles Here
For Economy of
Construction

Figure 28

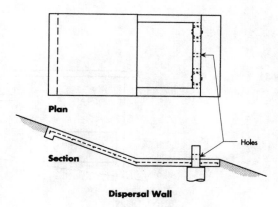

Plan

Section

Holes

Dispersal Wall

Figure 29

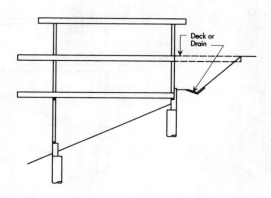

Deck or
Drain

Figure 30

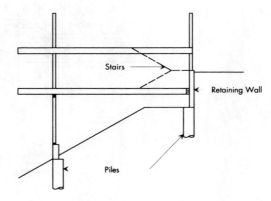

Stairs

Retaining Wall

Piles

Figure 31

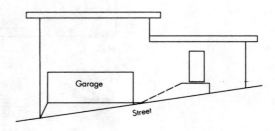

Garage

Street

Figure 32

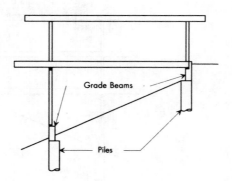

Grade Beams

Piles

Easements

On occasion a building can span an easement, but generally easements should be avoided. In particular, if power lines are on the property, contact the power company. An unrecorded easement may exist.

Deed Restrictions

These are the same as for flat land.

Pertinent Ordinances

See chapter 3.

Building Formations

There are seven main formations—as well as miscellaneous others—for the downhill house. These formations include the following:

1 One level along the street (figs. 32, 33, and 34). For example, on one of my projects the client wanted a design for a 22-by-46-foot, one-level house and an attached one-car carport on a 28-foot-wide lot that had a 45-degree downslope beginning 8 feet from the front property line. The client also wanted a 4-by-22-foot deck at the view end of the building. The space below the building could be unenclosed. Since the height above grade at the downhill end of the building would be 46 feet, construction would be a little difficult.

The design had the rafters and floor joists spanning parallel to the street and supported by a truss at each end. Each truss spanned from a pile 8 feet from the front (street) to a pipe column 24 feet downhill, then cantilevered 26 feet beyond the column. The last 4 feet was for the deck. The top chord

Figure 33

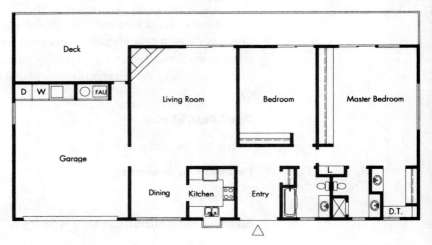

Figure 34

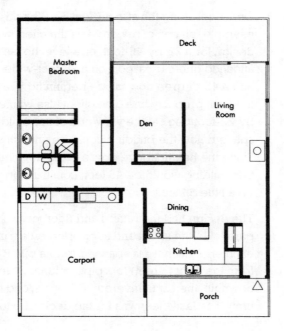

cantilevered to the front property line to support the roof of the 8-foot-wide carport. Since the height of the truss was from the bottom of the floor joists to the top of the rafters—almost 10 feet—the deflection at the end of the cantilever was small. The 26-foot cantilever was assembled with the aluminum siding installed, then lifted by crane and attached to the pipe column. The counterweight for the cantilever was the pile (fig. 35).

Another project required supporting an A-frame building 25 by 54 feet with the length in the downhill direction. The underfloor space was to be unenclosed. I designed steel V-frames supporting steel beams to support the building on four caissons. Lateral bracing was horizontal in the plane of the girders (fig. 36).

At another Los Angeles hillside area, I engineered eighteen Neutra-designed downhill houses. All were approximately the same size, and the underfloor space was unenclosed. I used tapered steel girders, supported by steel pipe columns and caissons (fig. 31). Wind bracing consisted of tie-rods placed horizontally in the plane of the girders. (The code now specifies that these braces must be other than tensile type members. They must also be able to resist forces in compression.) Downhill wind forces were resisted by attaching the girders directly to the foundation. As usual, each foundation was designed for a different depth of fill and topography. Pipe braces were used in lieu of downhill grade beams for some of the houses.

2   A split level, one half-flight above and one below tile street (figs. 38 and 39). For example, on an existing building that occupied almost all the available space, my client wanted an addition to fill in a small level area in front of the house and to wrap around tile downhill side of the building.

Figure 35

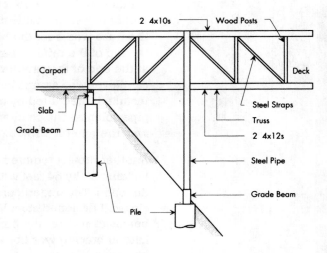

Figure 36

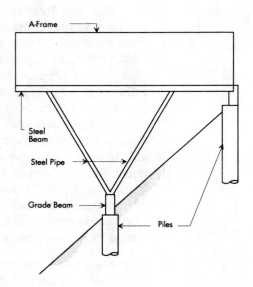

Figure 37

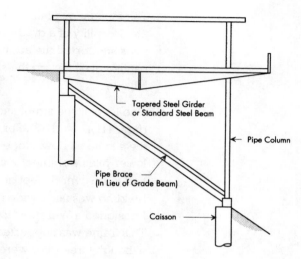

Tapered Steel Girder
or Standard Steel Beam

Pipe Column

Pipe Brace
(In Lieu of Grade Beam)

Caisson

Figure 38

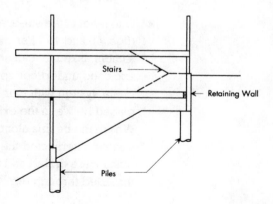

Stairs

Retaining Wall

Piles

Figure 39

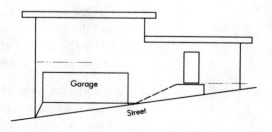

Garage

Street

The foundation plan shown in figure 40 indicates the flexibility of a grade beam-pile system. Four piles supported the addition by having beams that cantilevered toward the side and down the steep hillside.

3 One level at the street and another one story up (figs. 41, 42, and 43). For example, in one project, the site had a downslope of 60 degrees and the lower piles were near a cliff. Therefore, the piles had to be over 50 feet deep. Since the two-story building was fairly wide (parallel to the street), I designed a W-frame along the downhill edge. This frame was supported by only two piles, although three piles were used along the uphill edge (fig. 44).

4 One level at the street and another one story down (figs. 45 and 46). For example, for one such building a client asked that an addition be built within the enclosed underfloor space. I designed a grade beam system with four hand-dug piles that were placed between the existing piles in both directions. Where the beams along the slope (not the downhill beams) intersected the existing downhill beams, holes were drilled and the reinforcing steel was threaded through (fig. 47).

When the lot does not have a steep slope, and a high retaining wall at the front is not desired, the floor below street level can be reduced in width (toward the street). A retaining wall of moderate height can be placed at the uphill edge of this lower floor to increase the width (fig. 45).

The foundation support for a geodesic dome on a downhill site was another challenge, but the design I used was, as usual, a grade beam-caisson system.

Figure 40

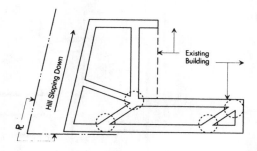

Foundation Plan

Figure 41

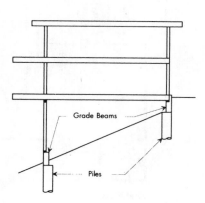

Figure 42

First Floor

Second Floor

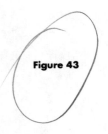

Figure 43

Second Floor

First Floor

Figure 44

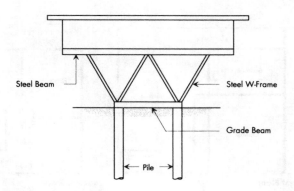

Figure 45

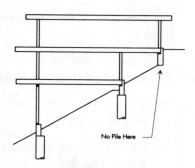

No Pile Here

Figure 46

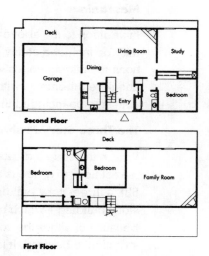

Deck

Living Room | Study

Dining

Garage

Entry | Bedroom

Second Floor

Deck

Bedroom | Bedroom | Family Room

First Floor

Figure 47

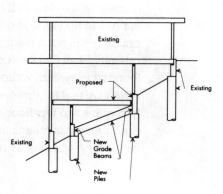

Existing

Proposed

Existing

Existing

New Grade Beams

New Piles

5   One level at the street and two stories below
    (fig. 48).

6   One level above the street, one level at the street,
    and a third floor one level down (fig. 49).

7   The garage at street level and either one or two lev-
    els below (fig. 50).

8   Other possibilities such as a building stepped down
    the hill (fig. 51).

Mezzanines

In addition to the above formations, mezzanines
may be included at any level. Because interpretations of building codes vary, it is suggested that you
check requirements with the authorities if a mezzanine is to be included in the design.

The Three-Story Problem

Where the code indicates that the space from the
lowest floor to grade is another story in height (fig.
52), a three-story building could become a four-
story building—which may not be permitted
because of either the zone it is in or the type of construction to be used. It is sometimes possible to
solve this problem by designing a retaining wall-
planter on the downhill side of the building to bring
the grade up to the required height. This way the
building will not have four stories. The grade beam
retaining wall can be supported from the dwelling
foundation system without additional piles (fig. 53).
Note also that for three-story buildings, codes usually require two top-floor exits, widely separated.
Frequently this means that an exterior stairway is
necessary, which is usually not permitted in a side
yard.

Figure 48

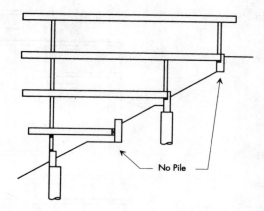

No Pile

Figure 49

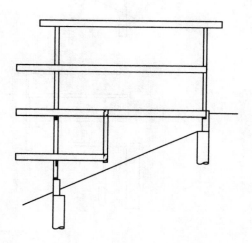

Figure 50

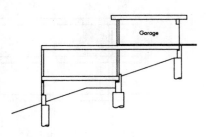

Figure 51

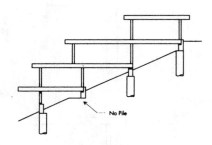

Figure 52

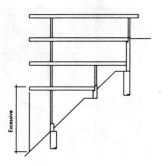

Figure 53

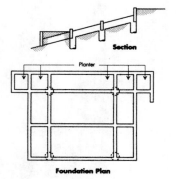

A property with a shallow slope will probably have
no problem using the design of one floor at the
street level and one above, or one with an additional
floor below. A steep lot will probably create an
overheight building if one floor is above the street
and the building has much depth away from the
street.

Effect of Sewer Depth

When a sewer is at a shallow depth, the elevation of
a lower floor is determined by that depth, which
usually means a split-level house or one floor at
street level and one above. If there is an easement
(or a possibility of obtaining one) through a lot to a
sewer in a street below, using it is usually better
than using a sump pump. Moreover, the architectural design is not limited as it otherwise could be.

Fitting a building to a slope by designing it to
follow the grade results in an excellent design (fig.
51). The objections are the number of steps necessary to climb from the lowest level to the street and
the problem of draining the roof to an acceptable
location.

Interior Layout

The interior layout of the building is the next consideration. It goes without saying that you should use
as much glass as possible to take advantage of the
view. Although special heat-resistant glass, double-
glazed windows, or structural steel frames add
some costs, they should be included if the view
demands. Opinions about the location of the kitchen
vary. Some designers prefer it near the front door at
the street side of the building; others want it facing

the view. Storage, utility, and bathrooms are usually on the street side of the building.

Stairs should almost always follow the grade; otherwise, you may need large retaining walls (fig. 54). Of course, where the floors both below and at street level extend the same distance toward the street, the stairway creates no special problem.

Fireplace and Spa

Because hillside buildings frequently attract romantics, at least one fireplace is a definite requirement. In addition, the recent trend toward hot tubs and spas means that the design should include the possible location for these even if they are not wanted in the original phase.

Decks

All downhill buildings should have at least one deck, usually along the downhill wall (fig. 55). For privacy, walls can extend from dwelling to deck edge at the sides of the building (fig. 56), or the deck can be recessed so that the dwelling is on two or three sides of it (fig. 57). The width of the deck should be 4 feet for merely walking out to see the view or for use as an exit corridor, 6 to 8 feet for sitting or sunbathing, and 10 to 12 feet for sitting at a table or for a hot tub or spa.

Where draining a lower deck is a problem, spaced decking, which permits water to run through, is a solution. A 1/8-inch separation of the decking is the best spacing, because shrinkage will eventually increase the separation to about 1/4 inch. Upper-floor decks can usually be drained to the street. Decks and/or outriggers have two other advantages worth mentioning: they make window washing

Figure 54

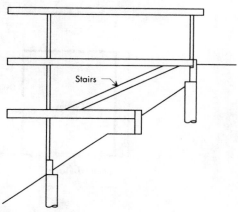

Stairs

Figure 55

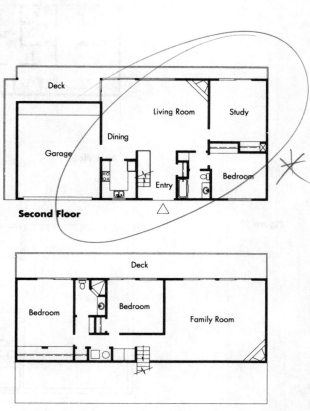

Deck

Living Room   Study

Dining

Garage

Bedroom

Entry

Second Floor

Deck

Bedroom   Bedroom

Family Room

First Floor

Figure 56

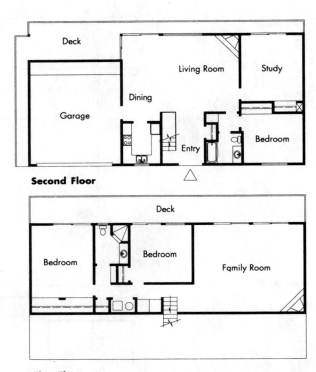

Second Floor

First Floor

Figure 57

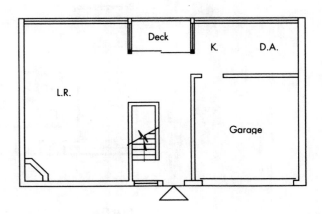

simple and minimize or eliminate the need for scaffolding during construction.

Bottom Floor

Where costs need to be kept to a minimum and codes permit, a bottom floor should be constructed even though no partitions are installed. Such a floor serves many purposes and it has considerable sales appeal.

Underfloor

Another necessary decision is whether to leave open or enclose the area under the building. If the area is to be open, the structural system could involve:

- Wood poles (fig. 58).

- Tapered steel (fig. 59) or standard steel beams (fig. 59 or 60).

- Glued-laminated beams (fig. 60).

- Trusses (fig. 61).

- An arch (fig. 62; structural by Paul Winter).

Two disadvantages of the open design are the need for special fire-proofing in some jurisdictions and its reduced saleability. Many people think (erroneously) that a cantilevered building is less safe than buildings that are enclosed with stud walls.

Building Shape

The downhill building can take many forms in addition to those previously discussed, including the Chemosphere house by John Lautner (supported by a truss system and one caisson), the arch house (fig. 62), the A-frame (fig. 63), the geodesic dome, and

Figure 58

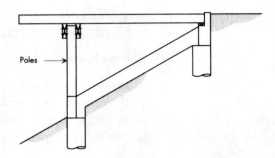

Poles

Figure 59

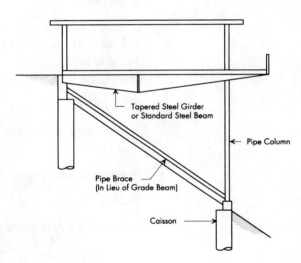

Tapered Steel Girder
or Standard Steel Beam

Pipe Column

Pipe Brace
(In Lieu of Grade Beam)

Caisson

Figure 60

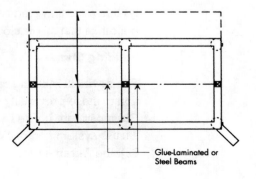

Glue-Laminated or
Steel Beams

Figure 61

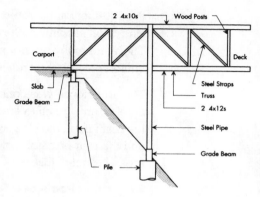

Figure 62

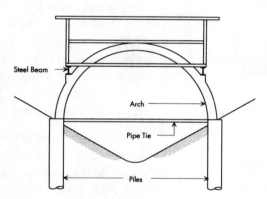

Figure 63

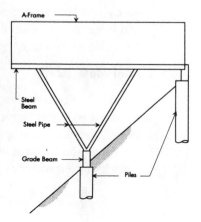

the 140-foot cantilevered house by Rolf T. Killing-stad, built recently in Spring Green, Wisconsin. There are many other forms; the possibilities are limited only by the architect's imagination.

The arch house was constructed to span a gully. Steel beams (cantilevered past the arch) support the main floor, the side walls supporting the roof and the rear edge of a mezzanine. The underfloor area was unenclosed.

Swimming Pools and Tennis Courts

Swimming pools and tennis courts on downhill sites are constructed in the same manner as dwellings. They are supported on a caisson or poured-in-place pile system, and may be open below or enclosed down to grade. Where there is insufficient space for a standard-sized pool, a lap pool with less width and depth than a standard pool may fit.

Tennis court construction can be concrete over steel decking over steel beams, with steel columns to grade beams that span to piles or caissons (fig. 64). Alternatively, the system can be concrete over plywood over I-beam-shaped wood joists, support-ed by standard timber or glued-laminated beams and wood posts, or steel columns to grade beams and piles or caissons (fig. 65).

Roof Materials

In the hills, fire-resistive roofs instead of wood shakes are generally required. Also, there is a trend toward requiring fire-sprinklered dwellings. Currently, the Uniform Building Code permits an extra story if the dwelling is sprinklered.

Figure 64

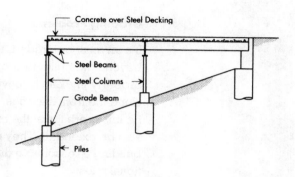

Figure 65

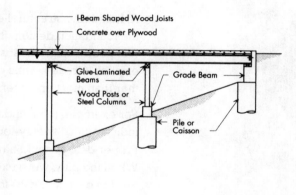

Figure 66

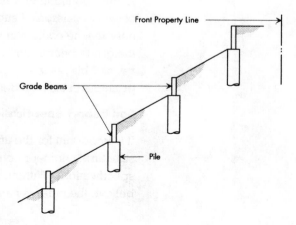

Grading Problems

If a lot must be graded, extending grade beams beyond the building proper and parallel to the front property line can remove the need for shoring along the front line (figs. 66 and 67). Other grade beams (perhaps at the rear wall of the building) can also be extended. They can cantilever from the building a reasonable distance, but may need additional piles.

Minimum Use of Caisson or Piles

Although the structural engineer is responsible for the foundation design, the architect should know that good design means a minimum use of caissons or piles. Grade beams can span and cantilever farther than most engineers expect.

For example, the foundation design for one project indicated that twenty-four piles would be needed. Proper design could have reduced that to only six. When the piles were excavated, water was discovered in each of the 30-foot-deep holes, making the cost significantly above what was anticipated. Another foundation was designed for the installation of twelve caissons. I suggested to the project engineer that he could eliminate five caissons, redesign the grade beams, and so decrease the cost. He revised his plans accordingly, then used the same principle in his next design.

Soil Report Specifications

It is important for the architect to coordinate with the structural engineer concerning the soils team report specifications. Without such coordination each may believe the other is handling these items.

Figure 67

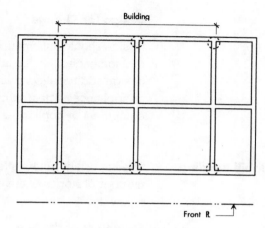

Figure 68

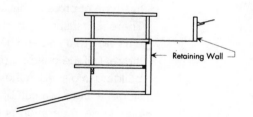

Figure 69

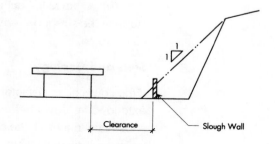

Design for Change

Design should anticipate change. For example, it is recommended that the architect incorporate into the design additional conduits for electrical equipment or appliances. These can easily be wired when the equipment or appliances are installed.

The Uphill Building

The important factors affecting location and the number of stories of the uphill building include the following:

Steepness of the Site

The steeper the land, the higher the retaining walls. Since these walls are a major construction cost for this type of project, this factor is the first to consider. There is usually one such wall at the back of the parking area, and another some distance back from the rear of the building (fig. 68). Generally, the building is placed in the area with the shallowest slope. If there is a cliff behind a building, there must be a large separation between the two, a high retaining wall, or both, and the geologist must indicate that the cliff is stable (fig. 69). A combination of soil-cutting and retaining walls is sometimes used (fig. 70). At times the authorities require that a steep slope at the street be reduced to an angle of about 45 degrees.

Soils and Geology

If the soil is not satisfactory and footings must be extended far down before reaching rock or other substantial material, the costs rise. Also, at times the soils-geology consultant or the authorities require the patio retaining wall to extend above the higher ground level—this is called a freeboard (fig. 71).

Figure 70

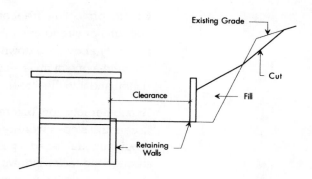

Figure 71

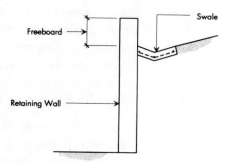

Figure 72

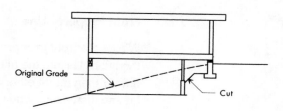

On one project the freeboard was neither high enough nor strong enough. A dwelling from another property above slid down the hill, struck an uphill building—one of mine—and knocked it off its foundation and into the street.

At another location, before larger clearances to ascending slopes were required, a mud slide struck a building, damaged a part of the back wall, surged through the rear windows, flooded the dwelling, then oozed out the front windows. This was not one of my projects, but I was called in to prevent any future problems of this sort.

If there is slate or shale rock, and if the planes are sloped toward any proposed retaining walls, pressures against the walls can increase considerably, thus necessitating stronger walls and, again, raising the cost. Any time grading can reduce the height of retaining walls, it should be considered. This is particularly true under the building (fig. 72).

On a few of my projects, there was fill at the front of each of the proposed buildings. The streets were also on fill. Caissons were needed at the fill area and grade beams at the front and sides of the garages. The side beams spanned from the front caissons to the retaining walls at the back of·the garages (fig. 73).

Front Property Line

Where the front property line is not at the bottom of the hill but is into the hill, the retaining walls must be higher than might otherwise be anticipated. A similar situation exists when a front setback is required by deed restriction, easement, or ordinance.

Figure 73

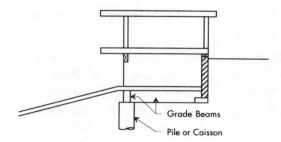

Grade Beams

Pile or Caisson

Figure 74

Cut or Fill Slope

Interceptor Terrace

Figure 75

Cut or Fill Slope

Diverter Terrace

Drainage Problems

Where a natural watercourse exists, either place the building out of its path, or have a civil engineer design drainage devices to conduct the water around the building to an acceptable location. Where large amounts of cut or fill are part of the design, the civil engineer must design a variety of drainage devices: swales, terraces, and down-drains.

- Swales should be installed at the tops of retaining walls, and the walls should extend well above them (fig. 71).

- Interceptor terraces are often installed at 25 feet on centers vertically (fig. 74) if the slope is to be cut or filled and is over 100 feet in height.

- Diverter terraces (fig. 75) are often used at the top of a cut or filled slope.

- Subdrains are used when fill is to be installed in a natural watercourse; they are placed in all flow lines leading into the watercourse under the fill and in the watercourse itself (fig. 76). Subdrains should discharge into nonerosive devices, as mentioned earlier and described below.

When retaining walls are not designed for the large pressures that occur, and when weep holes cannot be used, pipes must be installed at the bottom of the walls on the uphill side to conduct subgrade water away from the building (fig. 77). The soils engineer can specify where this drainage should be delivered.

Water from the roof, decks, and sprinkler systems must be routed carefully through nonerosive

Figure 76

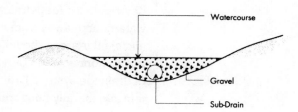

Figure 77

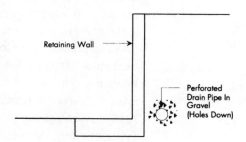

Figure 78

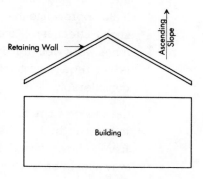

Plan View

devices to a street, drainage canal, or a natural watercourse away from the building. Building pads and similar areas should be drained into catch basins connected to pipes leading to the same type of drainage system. Drainage into a sewerage system is generally not approved.

When a building code requires a rear-of-building clearance and a retaining wall at the hill parallel to the building, I recommend obtaining a variance (if necessary) to permit the wall to be placed as shown at figure 78. Such a formation diverts mud, water, and sliding rocks around the building. To make good use of this rear clearance and to obtain the best view, place the living room, dining area, and kitchen at this level. A floor above could cantilever toward the rear to provide additional floor area. Also, it is sometimes possible to cantilever to the sides, and mezzanines can be included at any level.

Garage Access

When the street slopes severely, place the garage at the low end of the building (fig. 79). This permits maximum floor area and minimum retaining walls. If the approach to the garage is downhill along such a street, a relatively short driveway can sometimes work well (fig. 80). If a long driveway is needed the required retaining walls will boost costs considerably.

On a narrow street, access to the garage may have to be at an angle to the street, or the garage may have to be set farther back. The slope of the driveway should be as shown in figure 81.

Structurally designing a two- or three-car garage with the rear and side walls of concrete or masonry

Figure 79

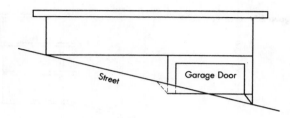

Figure 80

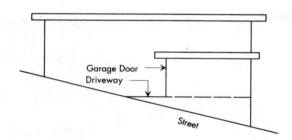

Figure 81

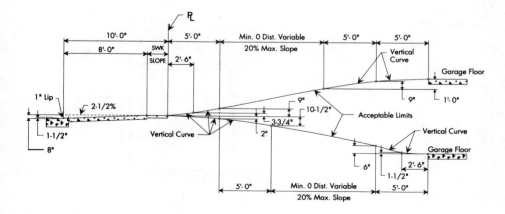

Figure 82

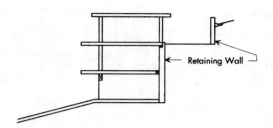

Retaining Wall

Figure 83

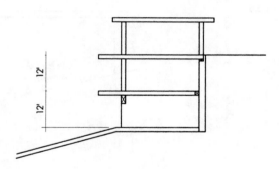

12'

12'

Figure 84

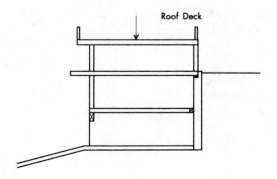

Roof Deck

can be economical. If the lot slopes steeply from the street to the rear, as is frequently the case, the usual method of construction (fig. 82) is to bring the building as close to the front as possible, and to build an approximately 20-foot-high retaining wall at the rear of the garage and another high retaining wall at the rear of the patio area.

If easy access is available at the rear of the lot (perhaps through an adjacent property), the dwelling can be constructed like a downhill building. Acceptable easements or a private street may then be required.

View

A good view is not possible from some uphill lots. If a good view is available, however, take advantage of it by doing one of the following:

- If zoning height requirements permit, raise the height of each floor (fig. 83), or step the building up the hill.

- Provide a roof deck (fig. 84).

- Place the dwelling or a part of it up the hill, separate from the garage (fig. 85).

Sewerage

If a sewer exists, there is no problem. When a septic tank and seepage pit must be installed, the layout for proper clearances between the units and from the dwelling can require moving the building farther from the street than is desired. On a narrow lot, the arrangement can be difficult to design. Also, the greater the distance between street and dwelling, the higher the required retaining walls must be. If the sewer is not in front of the development area,

Figure 85

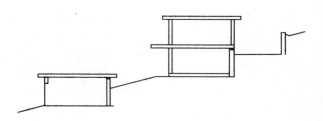

Figure 86

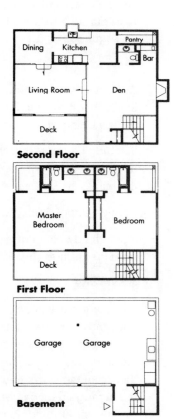

Second Floor

First Floor

Basement

the cost of bringing up a main line sewer can be prohibitive.

Easements and Deed Restrictions

Easements and deed restrictions affect a hillside project much as they do one on flat land. However, an unrecorded power line easement (established because the lines have existed over a period of time) can have an undesirable effect on a design. Specific clearances are required both vertically and horizontally from the power lines.

Adjacent Buildings

Nearby buildings can affect privacy, the view, retaining wall heights, shoring, automobile access, and building entry or egress.

Local Ordinances

Allowable height of building, zoning setbacks, parking requirements, rear-of-building clearance to a hill, and exit requirements are the most significant local ordinances. (See chapter 3)

Possible Designs (Mine)

One possible design for an uphill building is to place a stairwell in the front (which means that the rest of the building is moved back approximately 8 feet). This extra distance for the driveway approach allows the garage floor to be a little higher, thus reducing the height of the garage retaining walls. The 8-foot-space between the front property line and the main part of the building can be used for decks (fig. 86).

As an alternative, the garage can be placed in line with the stairwell and the balance of the building

Figure 87

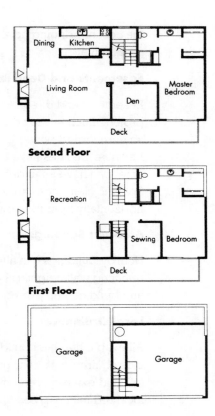

Second Floor

First Floor

Figure 88

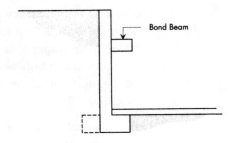

moved back a little, which allows the top of the garage to be used as a deck. An alternative is to incorporate the stairs within the building rectangle, which moves the building closer to the street (fig. 87). If the retaining walls become too high, the deck shown can be decreased in width.

On an uphill site, I placed a geodesic dome over the garage and bedrooms. Grading greatly reduced the need for retaining walls. Decks and a solarium at the living room level (the second floor) were a part of the design.

A few of my buildings were designed with bond beam retaining walls (fig. 88). The beams were inside the garage, and, besides lowering the cost of the wall, they supported the second floor joists. Other designs located bond beams at the exterior of the walls.

Elevators or Funiculars

An elevator or a funicular is worth considering. An elevator is not costly, and it has high sales appeal. A funicular can be used when the garage is at street level and the dwelling is up the slope to take advantage of the view. A dumbwaiter is also sometimes worth including.

Waterproofing

Waterproofing building walls adjacent to earth is essential for the uphill building. Asphalt emulsion is not recommended but Thoroseal and others are worth investigating. Also, install subdrains, covered with gravel, at the bottom of all retaining walls that are part of the building (fig. 89). These precautions prevent a buildup of water that could overstress walls or even penetrate them.

Figure 89

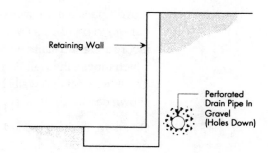

Retaining Wall

Perforated
Drain Pipe In
Gravel
(Holes Down)

Figure 90

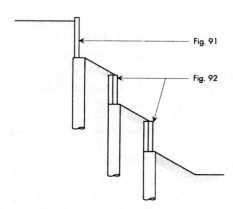

Fig. 91

Fig. 92

Figure 91

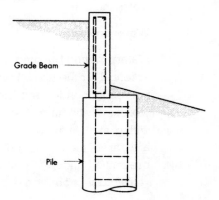

Grade Beam

Pile

Soil Report Specifications

It is important to coordinate the work of the structural engineer with the specifications of the soils
report. As noted earlier, the architect and the engineer could each believe the other is handling those
items.

Fire Control

Because of fire danger in the hills, the roof should
be of fire-resistive materials. There is also a trend
toward requiring dwellings to be fire-sprinklered. At
present the Uniform Building Code permits an additional story beyond code limitations if such a sprinkler system is installed.

Pool, Hot Tub, Spa

Frequently, a pool, hot tub, or spa is desired. These
can be located in the clearance between the building and the hill behind, but check with the authorities for clearance requirements.

Tennis Court

At one expensive property, my client wanted additional level space behind the uphill dwelling for a
tennis court. The hill behind was 60 feet high, had a
slope of 23 degrees, and was of unstable shale.
Shoring, consisting of piles spaced not more than
8 feet on center, was required, and the final slopes
could not exceed 26 degrees. A retaining wall system was constructed that consisted of three grade
beam-pile walls with 26-degree slopes between
(fig. 90). The top wall supported an existing level
area (on adjacent property) that retained new
backfill (fig. 91). The piles of the remaining two
walls had to act first as shoring then as retaining

wall supports (fig. 92). (See chapter 7 for a descrip-
tion of the construction.) The additional level space
attained was 74 feet from dwelling to the lowest
wall system, which permitted the court to be
constructed.

Fireplace

Because hillside buildings attract romantics, include
at least one fireplace.

Design for Change

Architects should, and usually do, design to accommodate change. It is especially recommended that
additional conduits be provided for the installation
of new developments in electrical equipment or
appliances. These can then easily be wired when
the new products are to be installed.

The Flat or Terraced Hillside Site

Buildings on flat or terraced lots generally sell for
more than those on uphill or downhill lots, although
the all-important view element can change the
equation. There is little difference between the
design of a building for this kind of property and
one for a flat lot. Drainage is to the street: the pad is
sloped toward the street, and roof water is conduct-
ed there through nonerosive conduits. Access to the
garage or carport is easily designed. Orienting the
building toward the view is no problem unless the
side yards are restrictive. The soil conditions, however, can drastically affect the project.

Figure 92

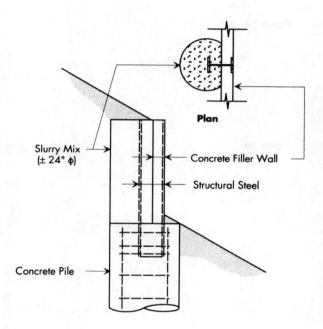

Plan

Slurry Mix
(± 24" φ)

Concrete Filler Wall

Structural Steel

Concrete Pile

Figure 93

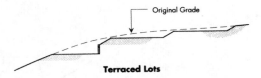

Original Grade

Terraced Lots

Figure 94

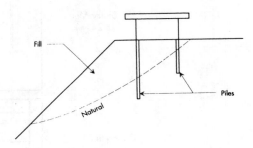

Fill

Natural

Piles

Figure 95

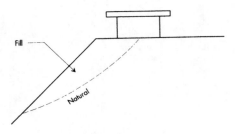

Fill

Natural

Figure 96

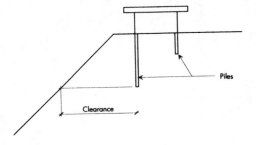

Piles

Clearance

Ground Conditions

Typically, there are three ground conditions for this type of property:

- Natural soil (fig. 93). Many lots have been graded as shown in this figure. Here buildings can be constructed on satisfactory soil by using the same types of footings as for non-hillside lots.

- Fill (fig. 94). The footings for a building such as the one in this figure would have to extend through the uncompacted fill into the recommended natural soil or rock below. Poured-in-place piles or belled caissons supporting concrete grade beams are used.

- Part natural, part fill (fig. 95). Some buildings, such as the one shown here, have been constructed using standard footings. The result was that the part of the building resting on the fill settled, and the damage was so severe that major reconstruction was required. With such ground conditions, either grade beams and piles or caissons must be used in the fill area or compacted fill must be used under the entire building.

Near a Downslope

When a building is near the top of a downslope, the footings must usually be deeper than expected; sometimes they must be piles or caissons (fig. 96). It is suggested that, if uncompacted fill remains under a building, a wood floor be used instead of a structural slab spanning to grade beams. This is generally cost effective.

Many buildings on flat pads are threatened by water-soaked earth sliding from the pad down nearby slopes. One effective way to prevent further

Figure 97

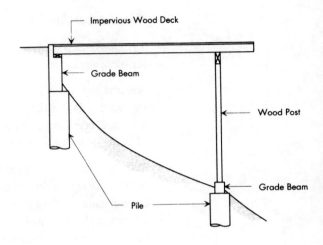

Figure 98

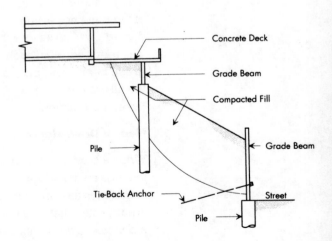

sliding is to use grade beam retaining walls supporting wood decks instead of large retaining walls.
The decks then conduct any water falling on them
toward area drains in the pads. Pile systems support
the structures (fig. 97). Because water can no longer
fall on the slide areas, the pads are protected, additional living space is provided, and the value of the
property goes up.

At one of my projects in Newport Beach, California,
a dwelling on a pad was endangered by a landslide:
a retaining wall and backfill were urgently needed
to stabilize the property. The top of the slide was
only 6 feet from the dwelling; the bottom of the slide
was next to a major thoroughfare. The design problem was difficult because the footing of the retaining
wall could not be placed into the street below, nor
could it be placed into the hill, where the excavation
might undermine the dwelling. In addition, the street
was next to the ocean, and the water level was high.
To solve this problem, a grade beam-pile retaining
wall was designed that varied in height from 6 to 22
feet. The piles merely supported the wall. Tie-back
anchors placed at one-third the wall height were
used for retaining. After the wall was constructed
and the 34-degree sloping backfill was compacted,
I designed a concrete deck to provide additional
outside living space. The deck consisted of a slab
supported by the natural soil at one end and cantilevered over a grade beam-pile support at the
other end (fig. 98). This additional living area over-
looking Newport Harbor greatly increased the value
of the property.

Code Changes and Existing Buildings

The effect on existing buildings of a change in the code depends, of course, on what is changed. In a seismic area, downhill buildings are not usually greatly affectèd by an increase of required seismic forces because wind forces normally govern design above the foundation, and ground pressures (retaining and creep) are usually greater than seismic forces for the foundation design.

Changes in grading rules can affect additions to buildings. If an addition is near an ascending or descending slope, the addition is required to conform to the new requirements.

If the new construction will add loads to an existing grade beam type of foundation, two things must be determined. 1. Has the code been changed to require greater depths for piles or caissons? Here a variance may be granted. 2. Will the foundation be overstressed? A structural engineer should check this, preferably the engineer who did the original building design.

7

Structural

Topography Plan and Soils-Geology Report

The first step in the structural design of a hillside building is to study carefully the topography plan and the soils-geology report. If there must be grading, study also the proposed grading plan because the grading can affect the location and height of retaining walls and may make shoring necessary. If it is at all possible to avoid shoring, this is the time to consider it. Stepping the grade upward at each line of grade beams under a building can at times prevent the need for shoring a street (fig. 99). Cutting the grade to reduce the retained height should also be done when possible.

For any given structural problem, there is rarely, if ever, only one solution. The problems of hillside design offer the imaginative designer endless opportunities. Keep your mind flexible.

The Downhill Building

Standard Footing versus Pile Formation

The inexperienced designer or contractor often thinks that a continuous standard type of footing should be used for a downhill building. Frequently this conclusion is based on a comparison of costs of standard footings versus grade beams and caissons or piles, a comparison that usually consists of computing the amount of concrete and reinforcing steel and the excavation costs for each system. But this is not all there is to it. For the following two reasons, caissons or poured-in-place piles should be part of the design:

The handling of the earth is not usually considered. Some jurisdictions do not permit throwing excavated soil onto the downhill slope. (The first heavy rain can cause a mud slide.) That means batter-boards to

Figure 99

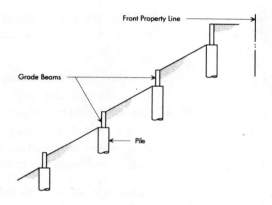

Front Property Line

Grade Beams

Pile

Figure 100

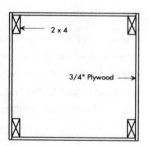

2 x 4

3/4" Plywood

Figure 101

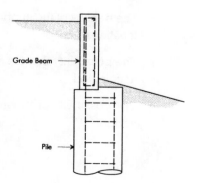

Grade Beam

Pile

hold the earth temporarily during excavation, then hauling the soil up the hill and disposing of it is required.

2   The irregularity of the slope of the underlying soil can cause a continuous footing excavation to vary in depth beyond the anticipated amount. Digging a deeper and deeper continuous trench can become dangerous—but digging a pile hole deeper than anticipated is not hazardous.

At one site, constructing a standard type of retaining wall on a downhill slope resulted in a dangerous excavation over 25 feet deep, and the natural substantial soil had still not been reached. The fill was replaced and four caissons were easily installed.

The choice of using caissons or piles is usually determined by the underlying supporting soil. If it is dense rock such as basalt, penetrating it with a friction pile may not be possible. In most cases, however, piles are the better choice.

Minimum Use of Caissons or Piles

It is wise to use as few caissons or piles as possible because of the unknowns involved, such as the following:

• The density of the supporting soil or rock at the location of the pile.

• The possibility that the depth of fill is more than anticipated.

• The possibility of striking water or an underground spring.

- The need to counteract additional creep forces (of the soil, downhill) sometimes required by the authorities or the soils-geology report.

Use four piles wherever possible. Grade beams are relatively easy to construct, can be increased in depth to span farther, and can be cantilevered a considerable distance. Large front-wall retaining forces can mean additional piles along the front, but not necessarily elsewhere. For example, the front line might need five piles, but only two might be needed along a line below.

·The capability of a grade beam-pile system to resist large forces was clearly illustrated at one of my projects in Hollywood above the Sunset Strip. An 8-inch water main in the hills broke one night. After two hours the water was shut off. In the meantime, all the fill of the street in which the water main was located and on the hill below was washed away. A downhill house in the path of the mud flow had its piles exposed down to the rock surface, but even though the mud pressure was significant, the building was left undamaged. The next morning we could see the front grade beam supporting broken portions of the concrete driveway, which no longer rested on the ground.

Pile Diameter A good diameter for piles is 30 inches. They can be either drilled or hand-dug and are usually strong enough to resist all forces required. When hand-dug, 32-inch-square plywood boxes can easily be constructed for shoring, and square piles (instead of round) may be more economical (fig. 100).

Figure 102

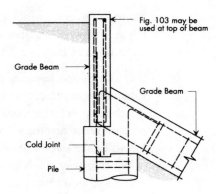

Figure 103

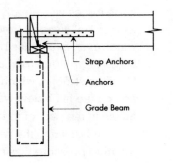

Figure 104

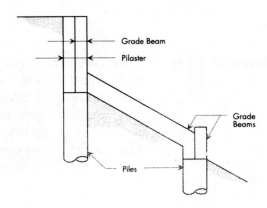

Retaining Grade Beams

Using grade beams as retaining walls is standard practice for my designs. All that is necessary is additional steel along the downhill face for beams with a simple span, and some at the uphill face for continuous beams. The beams, usually 12 inches wide, span horizontally to the piles, where vertical steel extending upward is used to resist the forces at those locations; if the shear is too great, a pilaster at the pile can be poured with the wall (figs. 101, 102, and 104). Some engineers use a 24-inch-by-24-inch grade beam-to support a block retaining wall (fig. 105), but the torsion of such a grade beam is excessive for a system using few piles unless the wall has a small height. If it is small, a 12-inch-thick grade beam can resist the necessary forces better, and only one trade is involved. (Fig. 103) Because the strap anchors are so important, inspection of these units should be required before the plywood flooring is installed. It is difficult to check them from below the floor.

Planning the Foundation

The first step in designing the foundation system is to plan the location of the grade beams and consider the effect of those that are retaining. Where any part of a retaining grade beam will be surcharged by a street, the additional pressure requirements should be determined by contacting the authorities. (Soil-geology reports rarely include this information.) On occasion, these beams extend beyond the area of the building, to retain soil. The next step is to determine the placement of the piles—again, using as few as possible (fig. 106).

Now determine the finish elevations on each side of each grade beam (including the beams running down the sides of the building). Although the details in this book show the bottoms of grade beams at grade, perimeter beams should be at least 12" below exterior finish grade. The retaining wall heights are then known. Generally, 12-inch-wide beams can be designed to resist all

Figure 105

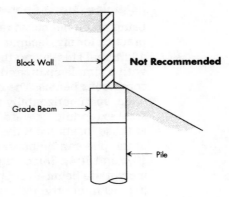

Figure 106

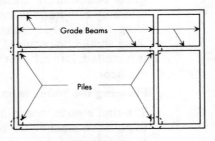

Foundation Plan

Figure 107

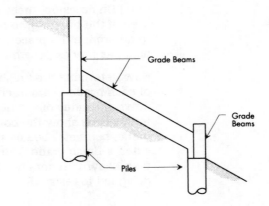

forces: retaining, wind, and seismic. The needed
resistances are not combined, however; whichever
force causes the largest stresses is used. When the
rigid frames are designed, creep forces applied to
the piles are combined with retaining forces acting
on the grade beams, but wind or seismic forces are
not added to these. If wind or seismic forces are
larger than creep plus retaining, then the wind or
seismic is used. The downhill grade beams are
sometimes made 16 inches wide.

Pile Ties

Piles that are part of the building are tied in each
direction, using either grade beams or structural
steel members (fig. 107). In addition to vertical
loads, these members are required to resist, in tension or compression, 10 percent of the pile loads.
Piles supporting retaining grade beams beyond the
building are designed using the flagpole method
and need not be tied (fig. 108).

When concrete tie-beams are used (fig. 109, which
includes references to figs. 110, 111 and 112), piles
that are tied together are designed as rigid frames.
If the frames are considered fixed at the bottom of
the piles, the moments at the bottoms are resisted
using the flagpole method. If, instead of being
designed as frames, the piles are designed using
the flagpole method, the interconnecting beams
must be able to resist their share of the moments
that, desired or not, occur at the tops of the piles.
These moments can be ignored if steel members
are used. Some jurisdictions require special approval for such members, but approval will usually
be given.

Figure 108

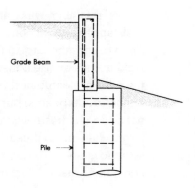

Grade Beam

Pile

Figure 109

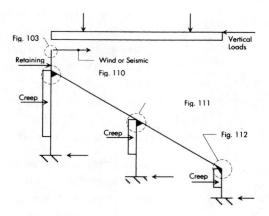

Fig. 103

Retaining

Creep

Vertical Loads

Wind or Seismic

Fig. 110

Fig. 111

Creep

Fig. 112

Creep

Figure 110

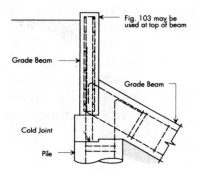

Fig. 103 may be used at top of beam

Grade Beam

Grade Beam

Cold Joint

Pile

Figure 111

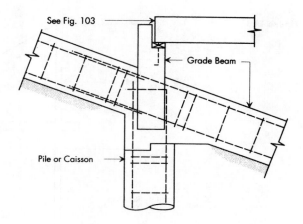

See Fig. 103

Grade Beam

Pile or Caisson

Figure 112

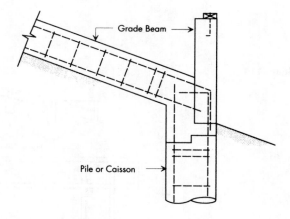

Grade Beam

Pile or Caisson

Figure 113

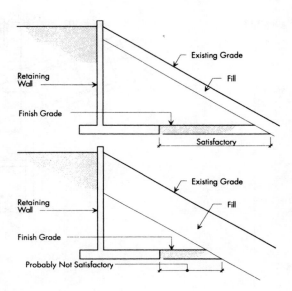

Figure 114

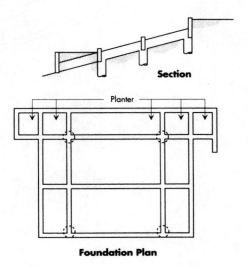

Section

Foundation Plan

Retaining Front Wall

If the building has a floor below street level that extends to the front, and if the quantity of fill is small, sometimes the required excavation permits the use of a standard retaining wall (fig. 113). On the other hand, if there is 8 or 10 feet of fill, the toe of the footing will not be far from the junction of the fill and natural ground, and often the footing will need to be deeper or a grade beam-pile (or caisson) system will have to be used.

Supporting a Downhill Planter

When, to reduce the number of stories, an architect adds a planter on the downhill side of a building (see chapter 6, The Three-Story Problem), I have supported the retaining structure (grade beams) by extending the downhill grade beams and cantilevering them beyond the building (fig. 114).

Floor Framing and Ties

Usually the floor joists of a building can be framed in the downhill direction rather than parallel to the front of the building. The advantage is that these joists can then be connected by straps directly to the foundation at each level (fig. 115), thus eliminating the need for shear walls in the downhill direction below these strapped floors and avoiding the requirement for vertical distribution of seismic forces in the downhill direction. This method also produces a stronger and less costly design. When shear walls are used over the downhill beams at the building sides, the shear of the plywood wall along the hold-down at the upper end of the wall may be excessive (fig. 116). The tops and bottoms of shear walls should be detailed; a standard type of detail showing either a rafter or a floor joist is acceptable.

Figure 115

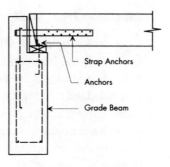

Strap Anchors

Anchors

Grade Beam

Figure 116

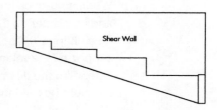

Shear Wall

Figure 117

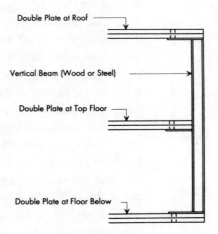

Double Plate at Roof

Vertical Beam (Wood or Steel)

Double Plate at Top Floor

Double Plate at Floor Below

On one of my projects a shear wall was carefully installed with proper nailing, drag strut, and hold-downs, but the top was connected to a ceiling joist. There were no connections from the roof (which was 5 feet above) to the ceiling joist, so the wall had little value.

Framing the View Wall

The architect naturally wants to take full advantage of the view by using as little wall as possible at the downhill side of the building, and structural design can usually accommodate him. If there is to be only glass at the top floor view wall, one or more vertical beams can extend from the floor below and cantilever upward to the roof (fig. 117). Sometimes the roof diaphragm can cantilever (not using rotation) from a wall a reasonable distance back from the view wall, or a standard steel frame consisting of a beam and one or more columns can be used. This kind of frame can also be inverted at a window (fig. 118).

Wind Effects

- Frequently wind forces in the hills are stronger than expected, and I therefore recommend the following:

- Use increased wind forces in the design.

- Use simple sheet metal connectors for rafter hold-downs, because uplift forces can remove roofs.

- Use light-gage steel straps around the corners of the building at each level.

- Carefully check any wood 4-by-4s between large glass openings as well as their top and bottom connections; they are frequently inadequate for wind forces perpendicular to the wall.

Figure 118

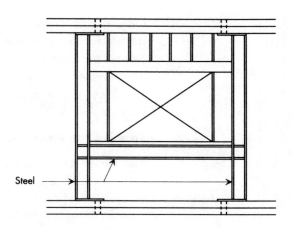

Steel

Figure 119

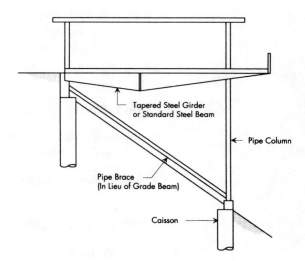

Tapered Steel Girder
or Standard Steel Beam

Pipe Column

Pipe Brace
(In Lieu of Grade Beam)

Caisson

- Tell the architect if there are to be large deflections of frames or shear walls so that he or she can better design the edge supports of large windows or use tempered or similar safety glass.

Open Underfloor Systems

When the underfloor space of the building is to be open (the cantilevered building), the engineer can select from a wide variety of structural systems:

- Standard structural steel (fig. 119 or 120).

- Tapered steel girders (fig. 119).

- Glued-laminated beams (fig. 120).

- Truss (fig. 121).

- V-frame (fig. 122).

- W-frame of steel (fig. 123).

- Arch (fig. 124).

- Wood poles (fig. 125).

Shrinkage, Drying, and Deflection

Because downhill buildings are often three stories high, and the underfloor studs are long on the downhill side compared to those on the uphill side, wood shrinkage must be given special consideration. If ignored, the accumulated shrinkage of floor joists can break piping. Also, the floors will slope down toward the view. Using special creative details (fig. 126), I-beam-shaped wood joists or kiln-dried lumber can eliminate this problem.

It is also suggested that you *not* use 8-by-14-inch and 8-by-16-inch lumber. Not only is it difficult to handle, but it can dry out, split, and fail when

Figure 120

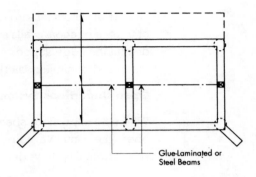

Glue-Laminated or
Steel Beams

Figure 121

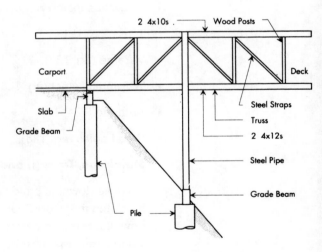

2 4x10s ———— Wood Posts

Carport   Deck

Slab

Grade Beam

Steel Straps

Truss

2 4x12s

Steel Pipe

Grade Beam

Pile

Figure 122

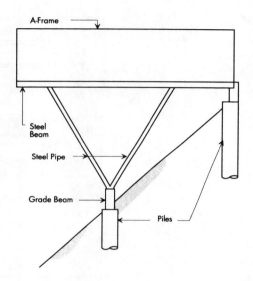

Figure 123

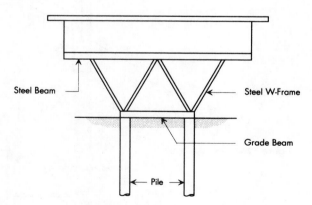

Figure 124

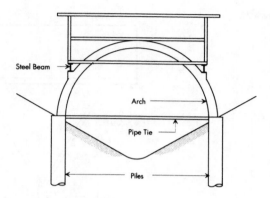

Steel Beam

Arch

Pipe Tie

Piles

Figure 125

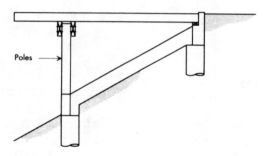

Poles

Figure 126

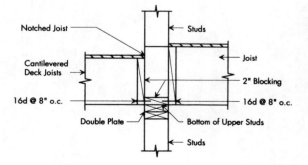

Notched Joist

Studs

Cantilevered
Deck Joists

Joist

2" Blocking

16d @ 8" o.c.

16d @ 8" o.c.

Double Plate

Bottom of Upper Studs

Studs

subjected to high temperature. A beam in an attic that is not well ventilated is a candidate for such a failure. It happened on one of my jobs. The attic served as an air-conditioning plenum, but not on hot weekends when the building was closed.

Except for building failures, deflection is the item that brings the most criticism to engineers. Sagging cantilevered beams and floors that feel "bouncy" are not acceptable even though their design may meet the minimum requirements of the applicable building code. This also happened on one of my projects even though I had overdesigned the joists.

Wide Openings

When wide openings are to be constructed directly above each other (floor to floor), be sure that there are sufficient studs as trimmers at each floor and below. The perpendicular-to-the-grain stress under the lowest floor could be excessive. The crushing of wood fibers can cause settlement of these point loads and allow the supported headers to break the glass beneath them.

Studs

To reduce the height of the studs at the downhill wall, it is sometimes possible to construct a double plate at a height that will permit horizontal bracing from that point to a grade beam upslope from the wall (fig. 127). This allows smaller studs and easier construction. The bracing can be members (such as 2-by-12s) at 4-foot centers, and they in turn can be braced (with 2-by-4s at about 6 feet on center) to prevent the 2-by-12s from buckling.

Figure 127

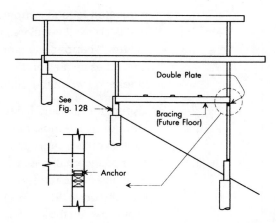

Double Plate

See
Fig. 128

Bracing
(Future Floor)

Anchor

Figure 128

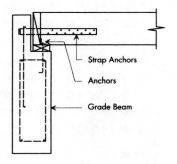

Strap Anchors

Anchors

Grade Beam

Figure 129

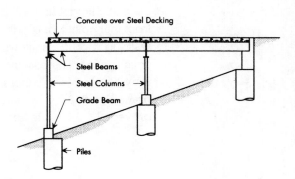

Concrete over Steel Decking

Steel Beams

Steel Columns

Grade Beam

Piles

Tennis Courts and Swimming Pools

Tennis courts can use the same type of foundation system as dwellings: piles, grade beams, columns, then either steel beams supporting steel decking with concrete over (fig. 129), or glued-laminated beams supporting I-beam-shaped wood joists supporting plywood with concrete over (fig. 130). I-beam-type wood joists to reduce the quantity of grade beams is also a method worth considering for hillside buildings (fig. 131). I have used this method of construction.

Swimming pools on a downhill lot are constructed in the same manner as buildings: grade beams and piles or caissons are used, with the space below the pool either open or screened with a stud wall covered with stucco, plywood, or other acceptable finish material.

Remedial Supporting System

A remedial supporting system was required for a downhill building, and I designed one. This building, with standard footings resting a minimum depth into topsoil, had settlement and rotation of the lowest footing, which, of course, caused distress in the wall being supported. To correct this, I attached a grade beam to the existing footing, using standard types of anchors, and the beam spanned to piles that extended into the rock below (fig. 132). This type of remedial work has been repeated on many distressed projects.

Figure 130

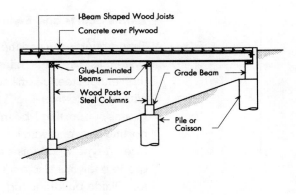

I-Beam Shaped Wood Joists
Concrete over Plywood
Glue-Laminated Beams
Grade Beam
Wood Posts or Steel Columns
Pile or Caisson

Figure 131

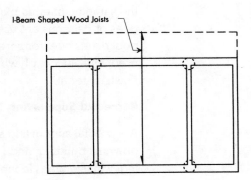

I-Beam Shaped Wood Joists

Figure 132

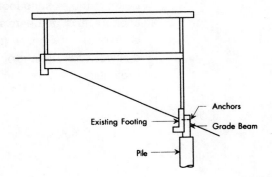

Anchors
Existing Footing
Grade Beam
Pile

The Uphill Building

Retaining Walls

The main emphasis for the uphill building, unlike that for the downhill building, is on retaining walls rather than piles. Shoring is also an important factor, however, and at times piles are required. The building design above the foundation is similar to that of the building in the flat lands.

Because the cost of retaining walls is high compared with total cost of construction, the success of the development can hinge on the skill of the structural engineer. Flexible thinking is essential in choosing the system of retaining structures to be used.

Retaining Wall Design

The items that have the most effect on retaining wall design are these:

- The soil.

- The possible need for piles or caissons at the front (street) edge of the building because of a large depth of fill. (Streets are sometimes constructed on fill.)

- The possible need to extend already high rear retaining walls above the high grade (freeboard), which would require additional forces against the walls.

- The possibility of the rear yard retaining walls creating surcharge forces against the garage retaining walls below.

- The possible need for shoring.

- The possible need for underpinning nearby structures.

Figure 133

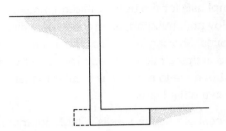

Figure 134

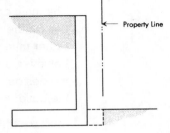

Figure 135

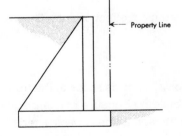

Figure 136

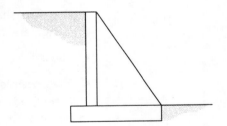

Figure 137

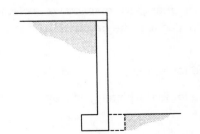

Figure 138

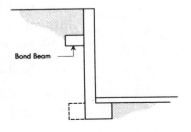

Retaining Wall Alternate Designs

For high walls, standard types (figs. 133-136) should be replaced, whenever practicable, with walls such as those shown in figures 137 through 142. Walls in figures 143 and 144 can be used if truck access is possible and if the authorities permit such construction for permanent (not temporary shoring) construction. The deadman (a solid block of concrete) used with the bond beam wall is another possible alternative (fig. 145). I used a deadman for more than one project to restrain a pile-grade beam frame (fig. 146). When tie-back anchors are used, the part that lies in fill or topsoil should be well wrapped (in much the same way that electrical conduits are wrapped). Water following the top of the natural grade can penetrate a cracked concrete cover, rust the steel rods, and cause them to fail.

Retaining-Shoring Wall. Occasionally engineering parameters (such as the coefficient of friction and passive soil resistance) are so small, or an equivalent fluid pressure is so large, that standard types of walls are unreasonable. In some cases the required footing key would be as deep as the footing width, as, for example, where bedding planes slope in such a manner as to create massive pressures against proposed walls. The wall shown in figure 147, although costly, can both shore and retain, eliminating the need for a separate shoring system. The construction procedure for this wall is as follows:

1 Drill the pile.

2 Place the pile reinforcing steel (which should continue up to the bottom of the concrete filler wall).

Figure 139

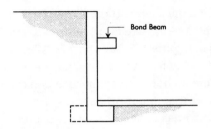

Bond Beam

Figure 140

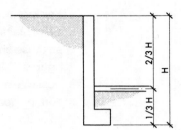

Figure 141

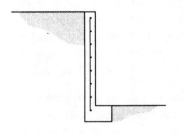

Figure 142

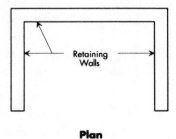

Retaining Walls

Plan

Figure 143

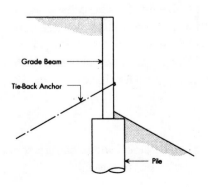

Grade Beam

Tie-Back Anchor

Pile

Figure 144

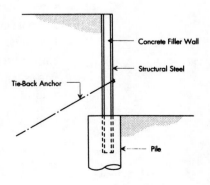

Concrete Filler Wall

Structural Steel

Tie-Back Anchor

Pile

Figure 145

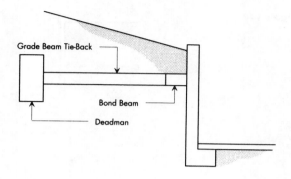

Grade Beam Tie-Back

Bond Beam

Deadman

Figure 146

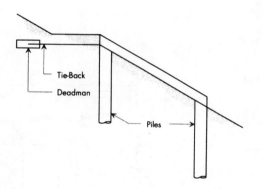

Tie-Back

Deadman

Piles

Figure 147

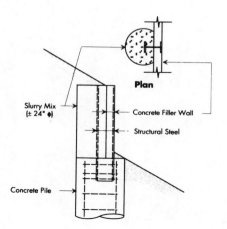

Plan

Slurry Mix
(± 24" φ)

Concrete Filler Wall

Structural Steel

Concrete Pile

Figure 148

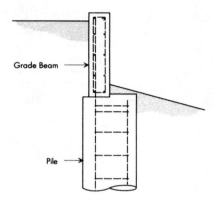

Grade Beam →

Pile →

Figure 149

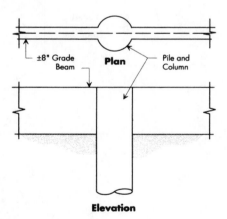

±8" Grade Beam

Plan

Pile and Column

Elevation

3 Place the structural steel member. (Make sure there are sufficient clearances.)

4 Pour concrete up to the top of the pile.

5 Place a sonotube form from the top of the pile to the top of the wall.

6 Pour slurry mix in the sonotube form.

7 Grade the hill down to the top of the pile and to the uphill side of the proposed filler wall.

8 Chip away the slurry mix from the downhill side of the sonotube to the uphill side of the filler wall.

9 Place the reinforcing steel for the wall. (It can extend through holes in the steel web.)

10 Pour or gunite the wall.

Where shoring would not be required, the use of the wall shown in figure 148 can be used.

Sonotube Wall. If the sonotube wall shown in figure 149 is used, the construction procedure is as follows:

1 Construct the piles.

2 Place the sonotubes over vertical reinforcing.

3 Place the horizontal steel through the forms.

4 Pour the round columns.

5 Strip the sonotubes.

6 Construct the filler walls.

Of course, rectangular columns can be used in place of round.

Figure 150

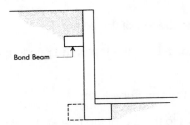

Bond Beam

Figure 151

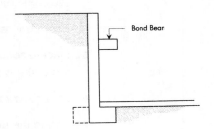

Bond Beam

Figure 152

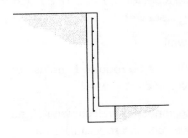

Figure 153

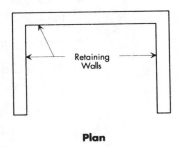

Retaining
Walls

Plan

Figure 154

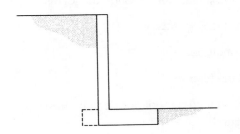

Figure 155

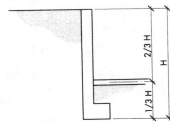

2/3 H

1/3 H

H

Walls with Bond Beams. The bond beams shown in figures 150 and 151 are used to reduce stresses in a wall and can span between cross-walls or buttresses. Beside a garage, the bond beam can follow the grade and be resisted at the lower end by the garage floor. If a buttress is used, it can have an extended footing (grade beam), which would probably require a key to resist sliding (fig. 164). (The wall in figure 152 can be used with horizontal steel spanning to cross-walls not far apart.)

Plate Design. Plate design (fig. 153) takes into consideration the actual deflections of a wall. A design using cantilevered walls (fig. 154) does not accurately consider the stresses at the wall junctions or the tension stresses at the inside face of a long wall. Plate design is covered in the U.S. Department of Interior publication (engineering monograph no. 27) *Moments and Reactions for Rectangular Plates.*

Garage Side Walls. Walls shown in figures 155 and 156 can be used at the side walls of a garage. For the wall in figure 156, using the frictional force (note its direction) can reduce the required footing width. This design requires either that the slab extend to another wall at the opposite side of the garage or that it be long enough to acquire sufficient frictional resistance. The footing shown in figure 155 is designed for vertical forces only.

If a retaining wall is restrained at the top (fig. 157), it must be shored until the slab at the top is cured.

Grade Beam at Building Rear

When a second floor extends a short distance beyond a garage in the uphill direction, a grade beam-retaining wall can both support the structure

Figure 156

Figure 157

Figure 158

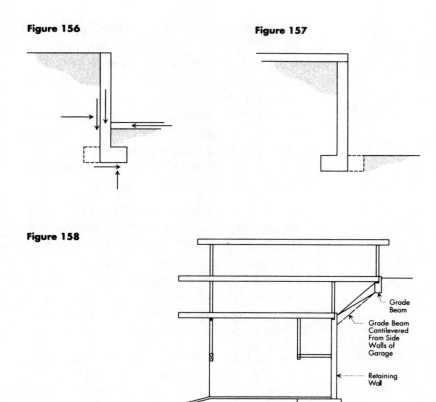

Grade Beam

Grade Beam Cantilevered From Side Walls of Garage

Retaining Wall

Figure 159

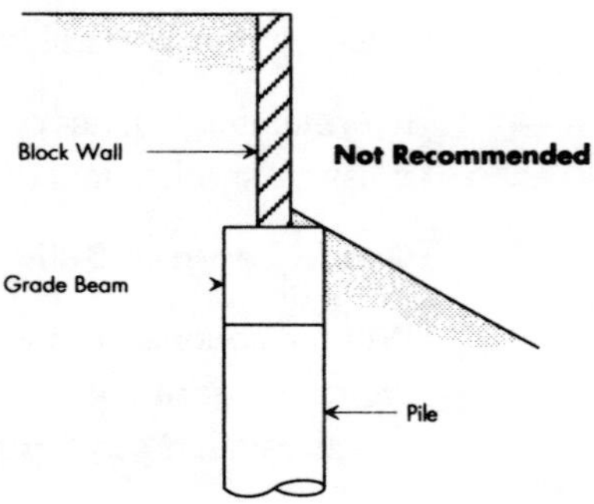

Block Wall

Not Recommended

Grade Beam

Pile

and retain the earth and can in turn be supported by grade beams cantilevering from the garage cross-walls (fig. 158). There are three advantages to using this design instead of providing a simple footing to support the rear wall:

- The simple footing does not need to be deeper than usual because of the sloping interior grade.

- The earth can be graded to reduce the height of the garage wall.

- There is no surcharge from the footing to the garage wall below.

Wall with Grade Beam Torsion

The wall shown in figure 159 is not recommended because of the torsional stresses induced. The wall in figure 160 (generally 12 inches thick) is far better. The retaining forces are resisted by horizontal steel in the grade beam. The horizontal forces at the piles are resisted by a pilaster above them (either in the wall or by increasing the thickness of the wall at the pile). The vertical steel at the uphill face of the pile can extend up into the grade beam (figs. 160 and 161).

Foundation with Grade Beams

If there is a large depth of fill or alluvium at the building site, a grade beam-pile system can be used for both the foundation and all retaining walls. (In such a case, study the part of this chapter on downhill buildings.)

When possible, it is generally better to build two retaining walls 5 feet high rather than one wall 10 feet high. The forces to be retained are cut in half, and costs are, of course, reduced.

Figure 160

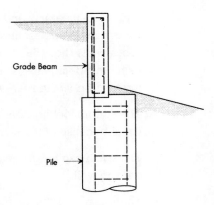

Grade Beam

Pile

Figure 161

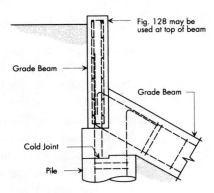

Fig. 128 may be
used at top of beam

Grade Beam

Grade Beam

Cold Joint

Pile

Figure 162

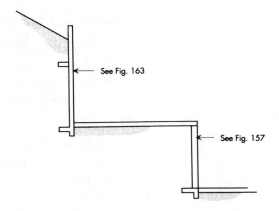

See Fig. 163

See Fig. 157

Weep Holes

Weep holes for retaining walls should be detailed to be above the lower finish grade and have gravel behind them. Otherwise, the finish grade may be constructed above the holes and cover them.

Wall Intersections

Where two retaining walls intersect at an abrupt angle, it should be made clear either by note or detail that the footings of the two walls are to be at the same elevation. Otherwise, one wall may be constructed and backfilled, and the other wall constructed at a higher elevation, thus creating an unacceptable surcharge.

Joist Anchorage

At this point, it is suggested that you review the early parts of this chapter pertaining to shrinkage of wood members and the anchoring of joists directly to the foundation. This tying of joists (or beams) eliminates shear walls and makes the building stronger. In the case of the uphill building, tying to the retaining walls generally creates no additional cost since these walls are designed for retaining, and retaining forces are not added to seismic or wind forces in the design.

One of my projects had a 16-foot retaining wall at the rear of the lower floor and another the same height 15 feet behind the building. This second wall had a 34-degree slope uphill from it (fig. 162); the natural soil was rock and had excellent resistance. The lower floor wall was designed to span from the lower floor slab to the slab above. The footing was small, had a small key, and the steel in the wall was reduced to one-fourth of the amount that would have been required for a cantilevered wall. The slab resisting the top reaction of the wall dragged that force to the bottom of the rear yard retaining wall, which spanned from its footing to a horizontal bond beam (fig. 163) that in turn spanned from a cross-wall to a buttress. A grade beam at the bottom of the buttress helped to resist overturning of the buttress (fig. 164). The grade beam was tied to the yard slab, which carried the horizontal thrust of the buttress back to the footing of the rear yard wall. This footing had a key that resisted all horizontal forces of the rear wall and the top reaction from the lower wall.

At another site, a landslide destroyed a dwelling below and threatened an adjacent dwelling. To protect the adjacent dwelling, I designed a slough wall consisting of horizontal, treated 4-by-12s spanning to vertical steel columns installed into concrete piles (fig. 165). The design protected a swimming pool a few feet from the wall, and earth from the slide could be removed periodically.

The Hillside Flat or Terraced Site

Major Factors

The structural engineer who is called upon to design a building on a relatively flat lot should be primarily concerned with the following factors: clearance from slopes, and the soil.

Building Clearance from Slopes. Will the clearances from ascending or descending slopes near the building cause a problem? If the architect is unfamiliar with hillside design, the engineer could face:

Designing a variety of retaining walls to provide the proper clearance from a building to an upslope.

Figure 163

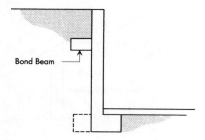

Bond Beam

Figure 164

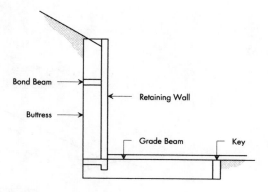

Bond Beam

Buttress

Retaining Wall

Grade Beam   Key

Figure 165

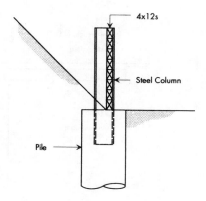

4x12s

Steel Column

Pile

Figure 166

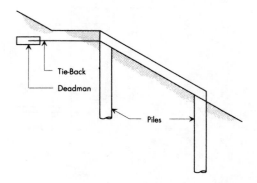

Figure 167

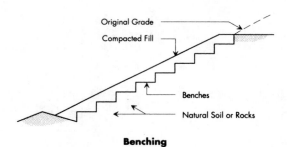

Benching

Figure 168

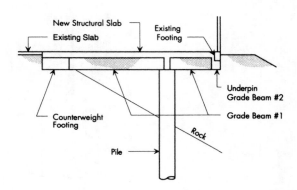

- Redesigning the footings near a downslope. These may have to be a pile and grade beam system if the building is too close to the edge of the descending slope.

Soil. If the building is to be constructed over an uncompacted fill, either all the soil under the building must be compacted and standard footings used, or the entire foundation must be supported on the acceptable soil or rock below. If part of the building rests on natural soil and the remainder on uncompacted fill, differential settlement will cause major problems for the building and the engineer. Obviously, a soils-geology report is as important for this type of lot as it is for the uphill and downhill sites.

Concrete Frame

If the foundation is to be a grade beam-pile system, the depth of fill (and the resulting creep forces against the piles) will probably vary. To reduce frame stresses, the piles can be of different diameters. I have also used a tie-back from a frame to a deadman resting in natural soil (fig. 166).

Building on Natural Soil and Fill. On one lot a building with a slab on grade was constructed with part of the foundation on natural soil and part on compacted fill. Toward the rear of the building the ground sloped down at a 34-degree angle. Unfortunately, the compacted fill had not been benched (fig. 167). The fill settled, and a crack developed along the natural-to-fill line. The settlement of the slab at this crack was unacceptable. I was called in to correct the damage and designed a grade beam-pile system to support that portion of the building that had settled (fig. 168). First, the piles went through the fill into the rock below. Next, grade beam 1 was poured with the counterweight footing and was extended to the exterior face of the building. Then grade beam 2 (supported by grade beam 1) was poured with a new structural slab. This procedure permitted new construction without shoring the building, although jacking was required to level the building.

Building in a Landslide Area. In another of my projects, a house in Malibu, California, was designed for a lot in a moving landslide area. Unstable earth existed down 20 feet to rock. A professor at a local university calculated that the horizontal force from the landslide could be as much as 2 million pounds. Eight 48-inch-diameter piles were constructed to support 24-by-36-inch grade beams. The rigid frames consisted of piles, fixed top and bottom, that penetrated the rock 20 feet, sufficient to withstand the calculated horizontal force. As an extra measure, the holes for the piles were made 66 inches in diameter so that the 18 inches facing the slide could be filled with a soft material. No forces from the landslide will affect the foundation until the landslide crushes those 18 inches of soft material (fig. 169).

A Word of Caution

A variety of methods and systems have been presented here to open the minds of those engineers who believe that for each problem there is only one solution. A word of caution is now called for. If at all possible, try to determine who will actually construct what you have designed. This is a lesson I learned the hard way.

A general contractor asked me to design a large home, swimming pool, and tennis court for a

Figure 169

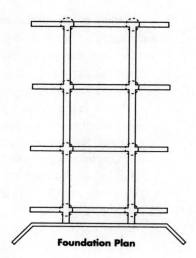

Foundation Plan

downhill lot. He discussed a variety of modern construction methods including tilt-up and lift slab systems, and was apparently knowledgeable. Many of the retaining walls discussed in this book were included in the design. In particular, a long, 16-foot wall was designed as a flat plate with tie-backs. It was later discovered that incorrect construction of these tie-backs made them worthless. Observation during construction disclosed that the job superintendent was the contractor's wife (who, it turned out, knew little about construction), and the walls were being constructed by inexperienced masons. The reinforcing steel was being placed without regard to proper location. In the 16-foot-high wall, steel was not at one face (as required), but at both faces and in the middle. Except for the wall cap, the construction of this wall had been completed. All of the water for the dwelling and swimming pool area had been discharged (unknown to me) not outside of this wall (as shown on the plans), but at the earth side of the wall. Since the downdrain had been incorrectly constructed, a large part of the water was deposited into the retained earth. As a result, the wall failed and fell onto a neighbor's property. Fortunately, photographs after the collapse clearly showed the deficient construction.

8

Construction

8

This chapter includes those items not usually considered for construction in the flat lands. Items routinely required for most sites—bringing in electricity, protection of the public, and having necessary toilet facilities—are not discussed here.

Removal of Foliage

The first step for the contractor is to remove unwanted foliage from the building site. Take special care where poison oak or ivy is present, and if construction might create any slides of earth, rocks, or building materials that could endanger properties below, build a protection fence below the building site.

Soils-Geology Report

Although the requirements of the soils-geology firm are supposed to be in the plans or specifications, they are sometimes omitted. It is therefore suggested that the contractor study the "Conclusions and Recommendations" of the consultant's report before beginning construction. In particular, any grading specifications should be read, and if maximum angles for cuts and fills are not included, they should be determined before grading begins.

Survey and Topography

Because of the usual irregularity of lots in the hills, the survey is of considerable importance for hillside development. Surveyors mark property corners and prepare a topography plan and should later be required to locate all piles, caissons, and retaining walls. The improper location of a pile can result in the need for foundation redesign and delay of construction. Also ask the surveyor to spot check the ground elevations to ensure that the original topography is correct. Foliage can sometimes prevent accuracy.

On one of my projects, an error in elevation of 6 feet required a retaining grade beam to be redesigned and its height increased by 8 feet—to 14 feet. Since the grade beam was to retain earth, the redesign affected grade beams and piles, and the change caused unnecessary delay in the construction schedule.

Grading

 When grading is necessary, it is generally best to do it all before beginning the foundation construction. If possible, use grading to reduce the heights of retaining grade beams or walls. The surveyor is, of course, required to set grade stakes.

Building Inspection

As elsewhere, the building inspector's first impression is a lasting one. Therefore, make sure that

- Excavations are deep enough.

- Loose soil has been removed from the excavations.

- Reinforcing steel is of the specified grade, neatly tied, and properly placed.

If these things are done, the inspector will probably believe everyone knows what he is doing, and further inspections will create few difficulties.

Reinforced Concrete Production

Hillside construction requires considerable use of reinforced concrete, so take care in its production. These points are particularly important:

- Carefully place and hold reinforcing in position.

- Take special care that clearances from reinforcing to earth and forms are in accordance with the plans. Moisture from earth touching the bars can eventually destroy them.

- Remember that the specified location and lengths of bar laps are important. Lap location is normally at the point of least stress; placement where stresses are high can lead to failure of the reinforced concrete.

- Do not use too much water in the concrete. The strength of concrete is drastically reduced if excess water is added.

The Downhill Building

Standard Footings versus Caissons or Piles

Instead of using standard footings for buildings on steep downslopes, consider caissons or piles for the following reasons:

- Today's code requirements for depths of footings on reasonably steep slopes are severe.

- There is usually fill on downhill lots.

- The irregularity of the underlying natural material can cause the depth of standard footings to increase much more than anticipated.

- Deep trenches are a hazard, and they frequently occur because of fill, topsoil, and the required depth for the footings.

Piles: Drill or Hand-dig?

To decide whether to drill piles or hand-dig them is
not generally difficult. The experienced foundation
contractor knows that setting up drilling equipment
on a sloping site is slow and costly. It is usually
cheaper to hand-excavate. Plywood box forms, 32-
by-32 inches, can be used for shoring fill and loose
top soil (fig. 100). Loose natural materials such as
sand would probably require driven piles. The
structural engineer should make sure this detail is
correct for the actual soil conditions encountered
and for the maximum anticipated depth of excavation. Where gases might be encountered, emergen-
cy equipment should be at hand. The soils
consultant should determine the possibility of
finding gas.

Wood Shoring

For poured-in-place piles or caissons, the plywood
shoring boxes (see preceding paragraph) are lowered during excavation and additional boxes are
added. One worker in the hole jackhammers and
shovels earth or rock into a pail, and the pail is
raised and emptied by another worker at the top. If
the piles are drilled, the density of the rock, where
rock is the underlying natural material, can slow the
drilling and require special drill bits. It is desirable
to remove all excavated soil from the site, or else
place it behind proposed retaining walls or in other
safe locations. Poor handling of soil can create
slides and lawsuits.

Excavation Inspection

Have the soils-geology consultant inspect pile excavations after they are dug and before steel is placed.

Placing Reinforcing

Reinforcing bars can be individually set into the hole, and the tie-bars can be placed by a worker beginning at the bottom of the hole and climbing a tie at a time. If heavy steel is specified, more and smaller bars are generally easier to install. If this procedure is not possible, the rebar can be tied into a cage that is then lowered into the hole by crane. Where the holes are did not too deep, the cage can be placed manually.

Grade Beam Construction

Next, the grade beams are formed on the uphill side, steel is placed, the forms on the downhill side are installed using snap ties, and bracing is set to keep the forms in place (usually only at the top of the forms, to stakes at the uphill side). Generally, forms of 1-by-6-inch lumber or plywood forms are used. Grade beams down a steep slope may require forms with tops and sides to prevent concrete from spilling out. (Portions of the tops are temporarily omitted for pouring the concrete.) Using pea gravel backfill is better than trying to use on-site materials that might require compaction.

On one of my projects, the contractor for a downhill building, not realizing that the grade beams could rest on the uncompacted fill, tried to treat them as footings embedded into natural soil. By the time his mistake was discovered, he had done a massive amount of excavation. He completed the foundation by forming the bottom of the grade beams, pouring, then replacing all the excavated soil.

Foundation Inserts

It goes without saying that making sure that the corners are square where they should be square is important for the framer. The concrete subcontractor is responsible for installing all inserts, including anchor bolts, hold-downs (with all-thread vertical rods long enough to grasp the hold-down properly), strap anchors, and so forth. These are of such importance that either the general contractor or, preferably, the framer should check their installation before the concrete pour.

Special Inspectors

The building code frequently requires inspection of grade beams and piles not only by the building inspector but also by a special deputy building inspector who checks the steel and takes samples of the concrete for testing. Where this is not required, it is recommended that you have it done anyway. At one of my projects (two buildings) it was found that after the piles had been poured, earth had slid onto them and was not cleaned off before the grade beams were poured. Vertical steel from the piles to the grade beams was already bent 2 inches out of line by the vertical weight imposed when this unacceptable construction was discovered after the buildings had been completed. The certificates of occupancy were rescinded.

Street Shoring

At times, shoring an adjacent street is required. If it is possible to close off part of the street and not install shoring, that is, of course, better. Otherwise, shoring must be installed before grading, and is generally designed by the structural engineer.

Water Control

During construction, do not permit any water flow from graded areas or the street to concentrate and create slides. Sand bags can be used to divert such a flow.

Piping through Graded Beams

Sometimes it is necessary to extend piping through grade beams. If this occurs, coordinate with the structural engineer to prevent problems of over-stressed beams.

Grade Beam Heights

It is important for the contractor to know that retaining grade beams must not be increased in height after the piles are poured without the approval of the structural engineer. Check the height carefully before pouring the piles. Just as it is not structurally sound to increase the height of a standard retaining wall after the footing is poured, it is not safe to increase the grade beam height after the piles are poured. The piles are the retaining wall footings.

Cold Joints

Coordinate any use of cold joints in grade beams with the structural engineer. On some projects, not only are there no cold joints, but the entire founda-tion—including piles and grade beams—is poured monolithically. This procedure is not recommended if caissons are used because loose soil will proba-bly fall into the caisson bell and decrease the cais-son's bearing capacity.

Wood Shrinkage and Underfloor Studs

Floor joist shrinkage amounts to approximately 1/2 inch per floor. Since this can amount to 1 1/2 inches for a three-level building, pipe breakage can occur. At the uphill end of the building some floors will be supported by the foundation rather than by stud walls, and shrinkage will not be cumulative. Where this is the case, floors will slope down towards the downhill side of the building. Using kiln-dried lumber is a possible solution for this problem.

Straps and Hold-downs

Many straps and hold-downs are used in the construction of hillside buildings, usually more than for flat land buildings because wind and seismic forces are greater and because there is more glass to take advantage of the view (and, consequently, fewer walls). These items are of considerable importance and should not be eliminated through neglect or oversight.

Engineers are frequently asked if 3/4-inch T&G plywood instead of 5/8-inch plywood requires edge blocking as is sometimes specified. The answer is that the T&G improves the resistance against vertical loading but, because of wind or seismic forces, it is not a substitute for the edge blocking.

Sewer Depth

Even though the architect may have determined the sewer depth (if there is a sewer), the plumber should advise the contractor of any problems with bathroom locations before construction begins. The need for a sump pump should not be suddenly discovered during construction. Other alternatives can also be considered if the problem is discovered early.

Slab on Wood Construction

When a concrete slab is to be poured over wood construction, take special care to prevent massive cracking. If possible, the slab should be divided into small rectangles. The concrete should contain only enough water to permit reasonable handling. The wetter the concrete, the more likelihood of cracking. If lightweight concrete is used, too much water can cause the aggregate to float to the top, and the concrete will be difficult to finish. Generally, lightweight concrete is not worth the extra cost and problems.

The Uphill Building

Main Concerns and Soils-Geology Report

The main concerns for uphill building construction are grading, shoring, and retaining walls. The soils-geology report should include the maximum allowable height of cut that can be made without shoring. Generally, at the top of this height, an allowable temporary angle of cut (steeper than allowed for permanent grading) is specified. For example, the report might specify that a vertical cut of 10 feet may be made and that a temporary cut at a one-to-one slope above that height is permissible. This procedure should always be followed if it can eliminate shoring. (Carefully explore the need for shoring and underpinning before doing any grading.)

Grading

On some projects grading extends beyond the area the plans indicate is to be graded, creating severe problems. If grading comes too close to an existing structure, underpinning may be required, which can result in a lawsuit if the structure is on an adjacent property.

Grading at the top of proposed retaining walls to reduce the wall height is standard procedure. If it is not shown on the grading plan, contact the architect for a possible revision of the plan to permit this cost-saving procedure.

Shoring and Underpinning

Shoring and underpinning plans should be included in the construction documents or obtained by the contractor. Improper shoring or underpinning can cause loss of life or property, fines, and delays in construction. When piles or caissons are required, review the part of this chapter pertaining to the downhill building.

Septic Tanks and Seepage Pits

When septic tanks and seepage pits are required, authorities in some jurisdictions require full construction and testing of the pit before they issue a building permit. If the test proves unsuccessful, either a main line sewer must be brought to the property or the project must be abandoned.

Figure 170

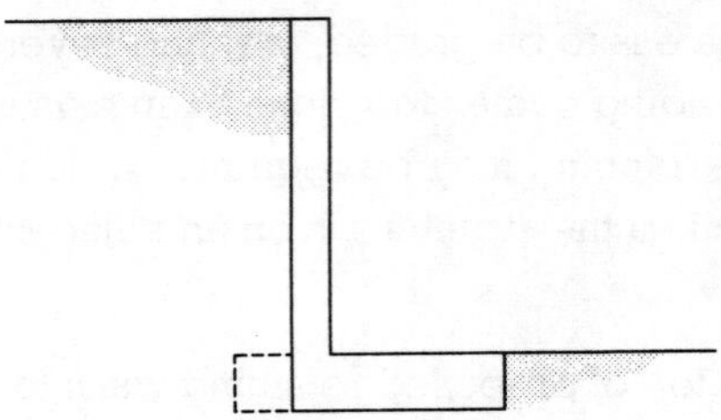

Figure 171

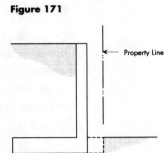

Property Line

Figure 172

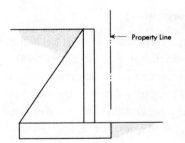

Property Line

Figure 173

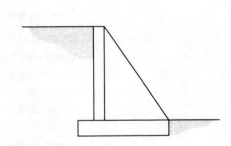

Figure 174

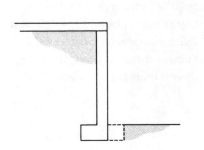

Figure 175

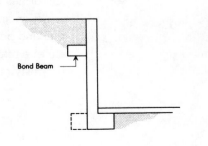

Bond Beam

Figure 176

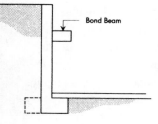

Bond Beam

Retaining Walls and Shoring

Most retaining walls are standard walls (figs. 170 through 173) and need no directions for their construction. However, those that are not simple cantilevered walls but are designed for resistance at or near their tops using either bond beans or slabs (fig. 174 through 176) may require shoring during backfill operations. This shoring should be designed unless the contractor has had experience with such construction. If shoring is not installed, the top of the wall can move horizontally. Short walls, of course, do not generally create a problem.

Gunite

Although the plans may not specify gunite (pneumatically placed concrete), it is frequently advantageous to use this material because then the walls do not usually need forming or backfilling. The strength of gunite concrete is high, and it can replace the concrete usually specified. The contractor can make the choice.

Drains and Weep Holes

Many contractors incorrectly install the drain lines at the bottom of retaining walls. The holes in the pipes should be placed downward to prevent them from becoming plugged, and the pipes should be laid with gravel over them. These drain lines keep hydrostatic pressure from causing water to enter the building. Weep holes are usually specified where retaining walls are not building walls, but even if they are not specified they should be installed, and gravel placed at each hole. Be sure that when construction is completed the weep holes are above the lower finish grade.

Placing Reinforcing

The correct placement of reinforcing steel in retaining walls, particularly concrete block walls, is important. Improperly placing steel 1 inch away from the specified location in an 8-inch wall can reduce the wall's strength by 25 percent or more. Steel clearances from earth and steel laps require special care. Vibrating the concrete while placing it reduces the need for repair (sacking and grinding of the concrete) after the forms are removed. The use of pumped concrete in the hills is standard.

The Flat or Terraced Hillside Site

The only problem with building construction on a flat hillside lot is the soil. The point is easily illustrated. Many contractors begin construction on such a site only to discover that the soil is not the natural soil expected. Sometimes when the excavation begins near the street, good soil is in evidence, but then as construction moves closer to the downslope, man-made fill is discovered. The digging can deepen until the trenches become dangerous, and sometimes only then does the order go out for a soils engineer. When the final results arrive, a decision must be made:

- The entire area under the building must be a new compacted fill, or

- The part of the building over the uncompacted fill must be supported on a grade beam-pile foundation system.

In either case, foundation redesign is necessary, time is lost, and a soils-geology report is necessary before design or construction of the building.

9

Cost Check List

The following check list is not necessarily complete for every locale. Not all of the items listed apply to all jurisdictions.

1 Land cost.

2 Land purchase escrow cost.

3 Survey and topography plan.

4 Soils-geology report.

5 Plans.

Architectural.
Structural.
Grading.
Landscape.
Civil (in the public way).

6 Energy calculations.

7 Government fees.

Soils-geology report review.
Pregrading inspection.
Plan check.
Permit.
Sewer use.
Hydrant use.
Park use.
School.
Driveway, curb, gutter, sidewalk, and other work in the public way.
Other.

8 Loan costs.

9 Temporary toilet.

10 Brush clearance.

11 Security fence.

12 Temporary electrical hook-up.

13 Soils-geology inspections.

14 Deputy building inspector costs.

15 Material testing costs.

16 Construction of building and structures.

17 Curb, gutter, sidewalk, and driveway.

18 Landscaping.

19 Landscape sprinklers.

20 Real estate commission.

21 Sale escrow costs.

Index

Index